September 26, 2014

To J.

Th... and sharing in our journey support ☺

TO DANCE IN THE RAIN

A Mother and Daughter's Journey of Hope and Healing

Hope and friendship...
priceless gifts to share!

All the best,
Clare Keating

CLARE KEATING

Foreword by Dr. George Lister
Chair of Pediatrics at Yale School of Medicine and
Physician-in-Chief of Yale-New Haven Children's Hospital.

CEITINN PRESS

To Dance in the Rain
A Mother and Daughter's Journey of Hope and Healing
Clare A. Keating

Published in the United States by Ceitinn Press
P.O. Box 1321
Middlebury, Ct. 06762
www.todanceintherain.com

Library of Congress Cataloging-in-Publication data
is available upon request.

ISBN: 978-0-9894652-3-6
LCCN: 2013949369

Edited by: Sue Ducharme – TextWorks EquiText
Book Design by: Karrie Ross – www.KarrieRoss.com

Printed in the United States of America.

To my Mom and Dad, Rita and Bob Keating,
who through their example taught me the
importance of faith, hope, love and laughter...
invaluable lessons to navigate through
my life's journey.

My Dad walked peacefully into the
arms of God on October 23, 2013.
I will forever love and miss you, Dad!
"Slan agus beannacht suaimhneas
siorai da anum" (Gaelic Blessing)

CONTENTS

FOREWORD

I WAS INITIALLY SENT A COPY of the manuscript *To Dance in the Rain* as a courtesy when the author, Clare Keating, asked permission to include my name. I was delighted to receive this book because I had an unremitting desire to learn what has happened in the life of Clare's daughter, Alicia, for whom I helped provide medical care just before I left Yale ten years ago. I never had the pleasure of meeting Alicia when she was a vibrant teenager before the tragic and heroic events described here. As I read, I rapidly recognized the power of this heartwarming, gripping and dramatic odyssey that portrayed Alicia's precipitous deterioration after surgery and her gradual and arduous ascent towards recovery. This epic, which recounts the patience and determination emblematic of the immutable bond between mother and daughter, would keep anyone firmly riveted to the book. That alone would have been enough to make this story captivating and compelling. But, this is also a text richly embedded with layers of important messages for the countless families who have faced life-threatening illnesses and injuries in their children and for the community of individuals assembled to provide medical care for these patients. To be sure, the reflections provided here are highly relevant to all of us because we will inevitably confront the loss or near loss of a loved one.

I met the author and her family under the most tense and terrifying of circumstances during Alicia's hospital course. As often happens, such an overwhelming episode can create and cement strong personal bonds that usually take years to form under normal circumstances. The sad and utter dependence on others that families endure at the time of a critical illness in their child exposes a myriad of vulnerabilities rarely shared with anyone but the closest friends. Thus, the responsibility of caring for a critically ill child and her family is a privilege that must be handled with respect, delicacy, privacy and compassion.

Through my lens, this compelling story of Alicia's devastating illness and remarkable rehabilitation highlights experiences that offer invaluable and empowering insights for families with a loved one suffering from a critical condition. A key consequence of the relationship that forms between parents and medical providers through the care of the child is the opportunity for the providers to learn subtleties related to the child's behavior, which may prove to be invaluable in assessing progress or the merits of particular medical interventions. It is in this realm that this book developed particularly special meaning to me, and one that I hope is instructive to the families of patients who are seriously ill and to all the medical and allied staff entrusted with that care. Here the book articulates some substantive lessons that are unique or at least rare to be expressed in print, and exceptionally worthwhile to highlight.

First, and perhaps most importantly, Clare recognized Alicia's responsiveness well before others, especially physicians, did. It is common for loved ones to detect neurologic improvement, despite denial by others, because they are well attuned to subtleties and spend far more time in direct observation. Hence, families often see this progress before nurses, and nurses before physicians. A change in heart rate, a slight squeeze of the hand, or even eye opening or blinking may be the first signs of a patient's connection to others. These provide the reinforcement essential to endure the long, tiresome and commonly erratic path towards recovery. And, the creative way in which Alicia's family used these signs to communicate and motivate is at the heart of this inspiring story.

Next, Clare acknowledges being welcomed into "medical rounds," that sometimes scary and almost sacred part of hospital practice where patients – the object of the discussion – are rarely asked to contribute and are often excluded from the conversation. Any patient who has longed to hear comments deliberately spoken just out of earshot or witnessed a discussion in the hallway that can only be seen, has expressed the frustration of this off-putting habit of physicians. The same treatment is often accorded parents who are serving as proxies for those who cannot hear or speak, because, of their illness or they are too young to converse. However, parents often have the most up to date, acute, and informative observations that are critical for understanding the responses and needs of their children. Regrettably, we often discard their observations just because we may not agree with the explanation parents provide. Fortunately, recognition of the value of incorporating families into the discussions is part of the driving force for the "family centered rounds" that are being adopted widely in children's hospitals. It is pleasing to see that Alicia's family felt welcomed. Their presence and keen observations were absolutely fundamental for guiding Alicia's progress.

Finally, there is a culture and bond that develops as those who share and help shoulder the fears begin to support one another. Whenever one feels despair or cynicism about the nature of human interaction, the observations of how strangers, who only recently met in a waiting room, or nurses and health care workers, who are doing much more than their "job", can provide comfort for those who are suffering, is exhilarating. Indeed, as Clare articulates throughout the book and reinforces so clearly in the Epilogue, that life has been forever transformed by the events Alicia and her family faced, but every bit as much by the community that surrounded them and brought "untold amounts of joy, comfort and happiness." Having a critically ill child is not the scenario one desires to test that thesis. On the other hand, this lesson may often be learned very late during someone's life, perhaps when the support is most valuable. These personal bonds are absolutely key for the healing process, and equally essential for the family's recovery with the loss of a loved one.

In addition to being an admiring reader, I am privileged to have been a part of their lives. I have focused here only on a part of the book, but the rest of the text clearly shows that the fortitude demonstrated by mother and daughter is emblematic of their entire relationship. In short, this is a story of one courageous and indefatigable young lady and her equally intrepid mother and family. This heroic chronicle is rich with refreshing insights that will resonate not only with those who have had a critically ill child but with all who confront catastrophic or seemingly insurmountable afflictions. The inspirational messages conveyed here should be stored for safe keeping as a source of courage when one does face tragedy and life's other formidable challenges.

George Lister

ABOUT THE AUTHOR

CLARE KEATING is a mother, a grandmother and an emergency room nurse for thirty years.

Her love of writing began in childhood, when she wrote and developed intricate journals. Gradually, short stories emerged that she shared with family and friends. Most stories have been nonfiction, all triggered by life events. Life's challenges have always provided topics to be expounded on or to find meaning in. Expressing them has become her passion.

She lives in Litchfield County, Connecticut, close to her three children, grandson and family.

INTRODUCTION

ON A COLD AND SUNNY SATURDAY morning in February of 2002, sixteen-year-old Alicia Townsend was rushed into surgery for the third time in twenty-four hours. She had just suffered a massive stroke, a catastrophic complication following a routine brain surgery the previous morning.

Alicia, an outgoing, loving, talented and intelligent high school junior, was a dedicated swimmer and had been voted to be the next season's co-captain. A member of the National Honor Society, she was also involved in the concert bands, track team and multiple volunteer organizations, including Venture Crew and Relay for Life. Offseason, she swam on a USS swim team at Southern Connecticut State University. Her life-long dream was to become a teacher.

On Friday morning, Alicia ran up three flights of stairs as her mom took the elevator; she met her with a victorious smile as the elevator doors opened outside the surgical suite on the third floor. Less than twenty-four hours later, as her mother hastily signed permission forms for the third surgery, Alicia's neurosurgeon, Dr. Duncan, explained, "I will try everything I can, but I need you to know that this is desperate. I do not expect her to make it."

To Dance in the Rain is Alicia's story—her fight, her triumphs, her setbacks...her journey.

Day after day Alicia fought with the help of her family and friends. At every turn along the path back from the very edge of death she pressed on, facing every challenge, inspiring everyone who observed her battle.

The dramatic events and circumstances described in these pages will impact every reader emotionally and inspire us all, especially those who are facing seemingly insurmountable odds, to forge on, to continue to fight, to never—ever—give up.

So many lives were touched as the circumstances of this story unfolded. Love branched out like ripples across a still pond, each bringing a new wave of hope. The cycle of giving and receiving is so much a part of our lives, the ebb and flow of our existence. Therein lies the beauty of our interactions with one another.

Everyone involved in any way with Alicia's journey deserves acknowledgement. I am eternally grateful to my family, friends and coworkers; to the doctors, nurses and staff who were involved in Alicia's care in various hospitals; and to all those who gave so generously, helping even in ways beyond our awareness.

Some insights and benefits came immediately; some were recognized in retrospect. All have been life-changing.

Most of the information in this book has come from my recollection, verified by those present at the time. I maintained logs of events, as well as journal entries. Many news articles were written and pictures taken by a variety of individuals.

The author also wishes to thank all of you who read this book; I appreciate it.

As a mother I have longed to tell Alicia's story, simply to let all who would read this know of her strength, courage and perseverance. She has fought and continues to fight the good fight. As parents we feel pride and joy as our children grow and experience life; we also share the sadness and struggles that our families endure when we are faced with new and challenging circumstances.

I invite you the parent, the fellow traveler in life's journey or the medical professional who cares and advocates for their patients, especially children and their families on a daily basis, to read and share in our story.

CHAPTER 1

Normal Day

NORMAL DAY, LET ME BE AWARE
OF THE TREASURE YOU ARE,
LET ME LEARN FROM YOU,
LOVE YOU, SAVOR YOU,
BLESS YOU, BEFORE YOU DEPART.

LET ME NOT PASS YOU BY IN QUEST OF
SOME RARE AND PERFECT TOMORROW.
LET ME HOLD YOU WHILE I MAY,
FOR IT WILL NOT ALWAYS BE SO...

ONE DAY I SHALL DIG MY FINGERS
INTO THE EARTH,
OR BURY MY FACE IN THE PILLOW
OR STRETCH MYSELF TAUT,
OR RAISE MY HANDS TO THE SKY,
AND WANT MORE THAN ALL THE WORLD...
YOUR RETURN.

~Mary Jean Irion~

MY THOUGHTS WERE ELSEWHERE AS I made my way through the main lobby and slowly glanced toward the front door. Exhausted, I looked up at the large clock just to the right of where I stood. Not only did I not know the time, I was not even sure what day it was. The clock confirmed it was just before midnight, and the dimmed lighting cast long shadows across the marble floor. There was hardly a soul in sight at that hour, but occasionally a resident or nurse would hurry through the foyer as they finished a shift to make their way home. The footsteps of the periodic passersby echoed against the walls of the empty lobby. The gaits of those few making their way out of work had purpose. I could almost sense that their day was not quite over; they walked with intention, as if things still needed to be done.

I made sure to avoid all eye contact with anyone crossing my path. I was alone in my thoughts, and no one was allowed into that place. Good or bad, I wasn't willing to share any of it just yet. Any acknowledgement of reality at that point would make what was happening real, thus needing to be dealt with. I chose to remain numb.

On a normal day, the constant activity in this area of the hospital was more akin to an airport terminal during rush hour. There were always the background sounds of laughter and chatter as families and staff gathered or met in passing, always a variety of conversations going on. At times they would involve detailed medical discussions regarding unnamed patients. Visiting families would gather as they arrived and departed. There was the constant clamor of voices and nonstop motion. Those were the typical sights and sounds of Yale New Haven Hospital, one of the largest and most renowned teaching hospitals in the country.

In the wee hours of the morning, silence was all there was to be heard. During those early days I can recall the sense of feeling utterly alone, even when surrounded by family or friends. A feeling of numbness had taken over my very existence during the past weeks; any escape was not likely to happen anytime soon.

I pulled myself out of that place back to reality, as I saw the headlights of the van making its way into the circular driveway just in front of the building. The vehicle, marked with the words Hospital Security, pulled up to the door. I was aware, as I had been many times in recent days, that I was consciously taking deep breaths, almost as if I had been forgetting to breathe. I sighed with resignation, picked up my bag, and made my way to the van. In a life that had otherwise become entirely unrecognizable to me, this nightly routine had become an activity that I could carry out mindlessly. I consciously dismissed any thoughts that drifted toward reminiscing about life as it had been just a few short weeks before.

Now my family and I were doing all we could to keep moving forward, figuring out what needed to be done and putting one foot in front of the other while trying to wrap our heads around the terrifying situation we had been forced to deal with. We were taking life one moment at a time while Alicia was fighting for hers.

"Hi, how are you?" and "Thanks, very much." were the only words exchanged between the driver and I most nights. I remained lost in my thoughts as we made our way from the hospital to the Ronald McDonald House about a quarter of a mile away. I had been staying there since Alicia's nurses and doctors had encouraged me to claim a bit of space for myself, even if for only a few hours a day. I knew that remaining at her bedside was taking a toll, but I found it nearly impossible to leave her.

As I left the hospital that night, as I had for the past week or so, terrifying fear and absolute sadness filled my heart. All of our lives had been changed forever, and I was becoming increasingly aware that I had no idea how to deal with this new reality.

Absorbed in thought, I passed through the door of my "new home" and walked up the stairs quietly, because everyone else in the house was usually sleeping at that hour. I opened the door to my room to once again wonder if this could be real. I returned here each night, yet it still felt so foreign to me. After I'd carried out the usual nightly routine, I finally stopped and was still. As my thoughts flooded in, I pulled the pillow toward me, hugging it closely and covering my mouth to hold in the feelings that were too much to bear. If I let the tears flow, I feared they would never stop; I would cry myself to sleep once again.

That night was no different from another. I prayed like I never had before. I prayed for strength, I bargained, I pleaded, but most of all I begged God to save the life of my beautiful daughter, who had been fighting for her life since a chain of events began which would plague our memories forever.

Again I thought, *If only this were a dream....*

CHAPTER 2

(Approximately three-weeks prior)

"Well, what are the odds...?"

"YOU CAN'T STOP THE FUTURE
YOU CAN'T REWIND THE PAST
THE ONLY WAY TO LEARN
THE SECRET...
IS TO PRESS PLAY."
~Jay Asher~

AFTER THINKING THROUGH THE DETAILS she had just been told, Alicia asked, "Well, what are the odds...?"

She was sitting up on the examining table in Dr. Duncan's office, dangling her legs off the side and swinging them back and forth. Any new thought or concern brought a question.

"There is about a 1 percent chance of any problems lingering after the surgery," responded Dr. Duncan.

"Hmm." She nodded to let him know that she understood. "One thing I really kind of worry about—is there any chance of me not being asleep? Like, how do you make sure that I am out before doing anything? Like, so I won't feel anything? Are you sure?"

With each question, Dr. Duncan smiled and gave Alicia a full explanation, taking every concern quite seriously. It was our second visit to his office. During the two meetings, they had developed quite a comfortable rapport. Alicia had a variety of facial expressions that left no doubt in the observer's mind what she was feeling at any given moment: a perplexed look of confusion; rolling her eyes as if searching inside her head for any concerns and questions; a frightened look of concern, usually followed by a full explanation of her deepest thoughts and feelings.

An MRI done about a week prior to the second meeting with Dr. Duncan had confirmed that there was a cyst located deep in her brain, which had just become worrisome. She'd had episodes of dizziness, increasing headaches and lack of balance over the past few weeks, which we had first attributed to her new intensive swimming schedule. Alicia had started to swim on a very competitive team following that year's high school season and the nightly workouts were exhausting.

After she'd had a few episodes of nearly fainting, Alicia and her dad and I decided something was amiss and took her to the doctor. A CT scan was done within a day of that initial visit. The neurosurgeon fit her in for an appointment within days. After a second MRI, the consensus was that the cyst needed to be removed. It was located in a bad spot and was beginning to interfere with the flow of cerebrospinal fluid within her brain. The surgical wheels were set in motion.

As was the case with many things in our lives, this became just one of those things that had to be done. Alicia and I talked a lot over the next few days about the situation, discussed the particulars with our family and prepared ourselves as best we could, for this detour on the road of life.

If you consider our Irish nationality you will understand how even brain surgery became the object of light joking. We posted a picture of Alicia's MRI showing the cyst that needed to be removed as the screen saver on our family computer. "Tumey," as it was called, became a term of endearment for a problem that wouldn't go away. Her brother Bryan who was fourteen, and sister Crissy who was twelve, were concerned right along with Alicia. The siblings spent many hours enjoying each other's company and offering their support during those days.

We had an appointment with Child Life to tour the surgical suite, as well as the Pediatric Intensive Care Unit (PICU), the operating room and the recovery room. Alicia's best friend Meaghan came with us; we joked, we listened and we checked out all the particulars. We walked through the PICU, a busy, large room that seemed warm and almost inviting. Yet it was just a room where Alicia was going to be staying for one night following surgery.

We toured the family waiting area and the sleeping rooms behind it. This quiet area close to the waiting room was the place where I would be able to sleep, so I could be close to Alicia on the night following surgery. Alicia asked more than a few questions as they came to mind. The Child Life social worker was as friendly and reassuring as she possibly could have been.

As we left Yale that day, we were all feeling much more comfortable with the events we expected to unfold in the days ahead. In their wildest dreams, no one at that point could have begun to imagine anything occurring outside the expected scenario. We were entirely accepting and trusted that everything was going to be all right.

As soon as I'd learned of Alicia's condition, I immediately took a family leave of absence from work, a decision I never personally regretted and in hindsight am ever so relieved about. From the moment we knew that Alicia was going to have surgery, I wanted to be with her as much as possible. I knew that even though she seemed "fine," and even said she was, it was still a huge event in her life. She carried on as usual, but her dad and I knew it was going to be a tough thing for her to go through.

Many days she would go and visit with her friends. After she came home we would sit for hours and talk. She never had any shortage of questions. As the date of the surgery approached, she would often insist that she really didn't think she needed to have anything done. "It's no big deal, Ma," she would say, "I'll be fine."

The initial anxiety gradually gave way to a kind of fascination with the fact that something very unusual was happening in her life. The fact that she was having brain surgery even seemed a bit fascinating to her. She thought it would be a good idea to take a lot of pictures before and after the surgery. Several times she even said, "Hey, maybe I'll write a book. Like, how many sixteen-year-olds have brain surgery?"

The three days prior to the actual surgery were long. Many hours were spent talking; there was not too much sleep. There were some tears and second thoughts. A few times Alicia did some serious thinking about abandoning the whole idea of the surgery.

Alicia was at school the day prior to the surgery and said good-bye to all of her teachers and friends there. She had a special fondness for some of her teachers and on many days would stop by their offices after school to chat a bit. Alicia was an easy kid to get to know and an even easier one to love. She was diligent, caring and endearing, always doing what was expected of her and more.

Alicia was worried about the schoolwork that she would miss and spent a lot of time figuring out how she would catch up with all of her subjects. Her teachers assured her that she had nothing to worry about. Mr. Ciarlo, her English teacher and track coach, made her very happy by giving her a box of candy. Alicia gave us all strict orders not to touch any while she was in the hospital. Mrs. Estrada, a religious education teacher at Holy Cross, also spent a lot of time listening to Alicia's worries and concerns, which really helped her accept what was going on.

As the countdown continued she frequently had friends over, and they as well as Crissy and Bryan relaxed, talked, laughed and took many pictures.

One night Alicia arrived home from Meaghan's house. Exhausted, she fell asleep early, but woke up around midnight obviously upset. She was very tearful as she told me of a dream she'd just had, of Poppy, my father, having died while she was in the hospital. This upset her as much as I had ever seen. Tearfully, she said, "Mom, I just don't know what I would do if anyone I loved were to die." Before that past week we'd looked at ourselves as a typical family, with all of the usual ups and downs for sure, but we were just doing and enjoying life.

Alicia, Bryan, and Crissy were all involved in a variety of sports and activities; a typical evening or weekend involved traveling from one activity to another to watch each of them do their thing. I was working 11 pm to 7 am at the time, which made it easier to facilitate all that they were involved with.

Paul was a dedicated "sports dad." He rarely missed any of the kid's games if he could help it and shuffled his schedule around to cheer the kids on at whatever meet or game was happening. It was no mystery where Paul was sitting in the crowd; he had no problem letting the kids (and everyone else) know where he was and for whom he was cheering.

All three siblings would frequently go to each other's games, cheering as well as enjoying the downtime with the brothers and sisters of the other players. Watertown Connecticut, is a small closely knit community where parents and their children enjoy friendships with each other from grammar school on through high school.

Academics were also a priority. After an afternoon of running around to practices, games and meets we would gather for a family meal. Afterwards the kids would hit the books and do what needed to be done.

Alicia was self-motivated when it came to academics. She was diligent, going above and beyond with everything that she did. We often found her up late at night working on perfecting a cover for a paper or project that she had been working on all day. She always did her best.

Bryan was doing well academically but had other interests that took priority for him. Bryan luckily found ways to get done just what needed to be done so he could continue being a well-rounded young man. He excelled athletically in any sport that he decided he was interested in. Bryan learned best from hands-on experience, so Paul and I tried to expose him to a variety of information; we traveled and worked outside the box to find ways to motivate his learning style.

Crissy was our adorable, charming social light, and a good student when just the right amount of motivation occurred. She was our fast-running and hard-playing soccer girl, always involved in local as well as travel teams.

In early 2002, life was good. We were adjusting constantly to the changing needs and circumstances presented to us; all of us enjoyed our interactions with family and friends. We each looked ahead to a future full of possibilities.

❦

I was brought up in a large, close-knit family; we had quite a web of loving, extended family around us at all times. My parents Rita and Bob, known as Nanny and Poppy by the grandchildren, lived close by. We all visited frequently and were an important part of each other's lives.

My oldest sister Mary had lived in California since the 1980s with her husband and daughter. I also had a younger sister Deirdre, or Sr. Mary Dolora as she is now called, who is a professed Catholic Religious in the Sisters of Mercy of Alma. She lived in the Washington, DC area and was working at the Basilica of the National Shrine of the Immaculate Conception at the time.

The rest of my siblings lived close by; we shared in each other's lives on a regular basis. Theresa and her husband Mike had five children. Margaret, who I call Margie, and her husband Brian had two; they were all in the same age ranges as Alicia, Crissy and Bryan. We spent many enjoyable hours together as the children were growing up. The cousins have been like brothers and sisters to one another and their closeness has only grown stronger over the years.

When major life changes happen to any of us, they affect all of us. We have always supported one another in any way we can, and we fight alongside each other as we deal with life's challenges.

Bryan, Alicia and Crissy following a Christmas Concert

Alicia with Nanny and Poppy following graduation from St. John School - 1999

"Well, what are the odds…?

Family & Friends

Family & Friends

Alicia in a swim meet in January 2002

CHAPTER 3

Swimmers, Take Your Mark!

ON THE MORNING OF FEBRUARY 15TH we made our way to Yale in relative silence, each busy with our own thoughts and fears. Alicia's surgery had been postponed the day before due to the unavailability of a bed in the Pediatric Intensive Care Unit (PICU).

We were running late as usual. It was about 6:30 am as Alicia and I made a run for the elevators while Paul parked the car. The two of us shared one last glance, filled with anxiety as well as the ever-present desire to enjoy every minute we could. Alicia and I had decided to have a race; as I pushed the button for the third floor, Alicia darted for the stairwell. I got in, and when the elevator door opened, Alicia stood there with a victorious smile. I gave her a quick nod and congratulations on a good run. Then we quickly made our way down the hall to the pediatric surgical reception area. There was no one in sight but we knew the setup, having been there the day before.

As we caught our breath and collected our thoughts, the receptionist arrived and checked off that Alicia was there. We made our way to the "best" of the four waiting rooms, the one with the comfortable couch and a television, and started watching *Good Morning America*. Alicia sat next to me, took off her shoes, put her feet on my lap and of course asked for a foot massage while we talked. She had not been the touchy-feely type for years, but she welcomed that source of comfort and relaxation.

Once Paul arrived in the waiting area and the three of us stopped moving, we all began to sense our anxiety. At that point we were experiencing fear and hesitation regarding the unknown and anxious at the same time to have it all behind us. None of us knew what to expect. The idea of brain surgery was another of those unfamiliar challenges placed before us that needed to be dealt with. As we'd tried to imagine having to go through something so scary, we'd quickly dispelled, rationalized, or covered up our thoughts and overwhelming concerns. I was very conscious of not wanting to make Alicia more nervous, so cool, calm and collected was my face of the day. I know...but we're Irish, that's how we roll.

As we watched *Good Morning America* and fit in a quick foot massage, Alicia had hardly enough time to get nervous. To think that we had actually arrived at this day, to know that my daughter needed such dramatic surgery, was unbelievable. The scenario was one that would have never in our wildest dreams crossed our minds even one month before.

Until the previous month, life for Alicia was very exciting. She was a junior in high school. Just two months before, she had completed a wonderful high school swimming season and became a member of the Naugatuck Valley League All-Star Team. She had always been a very determined young lady and that year was no different. She was very proud of the fact that she'd dramatically cut times in all of her events, especially those that she loved the most. She had qualified for the state trials in the

200- and 500-yard freestyle, as well as the 4x100 free relay. She had many close friendships, each cherished, and considered herself very lucky.

Surgical Waiting Area – February 15, 2002

At about 7:45 the anesthesiologists came and introduced themselves and led us into the recovery room. They sent Alicia off to the bathroom to change into the hospital gown. She took more than an adequate amount of time to do what had to be done. We smirked, knowing that her ploy to stall was quite understandable.

Within a few minutes the anesthesiologist started an intravenous line and administered a sedative, and we walked beside Alicia as she was wheeled down the hall. She was very relaxed at that point, which made it a bit less devastating to see my little girl being wheeled off to the unknown.

Within an hour, Larry the operating room nurse came out to tell Paul and I that Alicia was doing fine and that they had just gotten underway a short while ago. He came out again about an hour later to say that things were still going quite well and that Dr. Duncan had just started with the microscope.

I inquired whether Dr. Duncan had decided to drain the cyst versus taking it out entirely. Larry said he was not sure, he would let us know as soon as possible.

At about 11:45 both Dr. Duncan and Larry came into the waiting room, letting us know that they had just finished the surgery. They made a couple of light, joking comments about who cut hair better before Larry went back in through the OR doors.

Dr. Duncan explained in detail what he had done. He had removed the cyst entirely, and said that Alicia had tolerated the surgery very well. He also mentioned that this would be a good time for us to take a break. She would be in the recovery room for an hour or more; he said that he would see us upstairs in the PICU a little later. Things appeared to be going along as planned, so we had a leisurely lunch and took some time to talk over the events of the past couple of weeks.

We came back upstairs at about 12:45 and walked to the PICU intercom to inquire if Alicia had arrived there yet from the recovery room. They told us that she had and allowed us in. Alicia dozed for most of the afternoon, while several family members and close family friends stopped by for a quick visit.

Paul left at about six o'clock to go and pick up Crissy and Bryan at my sister Theresa's house. They had spent the day there with their cousins while we were at Yale with Alicia.

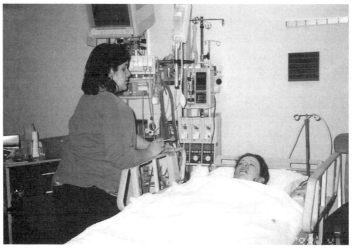

The PICU nurse, Jessica and Alicia after her first surgery on the evening of Feb. 15th.

CHAPTER 4

Minutes Turn to Hours...

ABOUT 9 PM I NOTICED THAT ALICIA was taking a turn for the worse. My sister Margie and my friend Fr. Stan had just left after visiting for a bit. Alicia's persistent headache was not letting up at all. She had been complaining of increasingly severe pain in her head for the past few hours; she was no longer getting relief from the pain medicine. She also started vomiting. What had appeared to be symptoms expected to follow that type of surgery gradually seemed to indicate that Alicia was showing some signs of increasing pressure inside her brain.

Her nurses continued providing pain medication and frequently assessed her changing condition. Helpless was all I felt; I was uncomfortable with not being able to do anything to help Alicia, who moaned out in pain whenever she drifted out of her morphine-induced sedation. Changes in her blood pressure and heart rate gradually became evident; each minute brought an increase in concern, which transformed slowly into fear. All perception of time was lost, seeming like nearly forever as we waited for the neurosurgery residents to come and evaluate Alicia's worsening symptoms.

Hours flew by while I focused intensely on her every breath accompanied by grimaces. I answered her questions and reassured Alicia that everyone was doing all they could to get her to feel better. Deep down inside I feared that something appeared to be going very wrong.

"Mom, can you rub my feet?" was a question that I'd heard often over the past weeks as the two of us sat and talked about all the considerations that she verbalized about her upcoming brain surgery. As the hours went by I sat vigil with my girl, holding her hand as she moaned out in pain and drifted in and out of consciousness. Whenever her pain subsided a bit I would give her a foot massage, helping her to drift back off to sleep.

The neurosurgery residents evaluated her and assured us that those symptoms were typical following that type of surgery.

The amount of morphine was increased. Alicia remained asleep and quiet for a bit, and I was encouraged to go and lay down for a while. None of us had slept well the night before, anticipating the surgery. I had to be assured several times by her nurse that she would let me know if Alicia woke up and asked for me, or if there were any changes in her condition.

I made my way to the family rooms just down the hall. We had picked out a room earlier where I would spend the night. The bed was all ready to jump into, so I just threw the blanket on. I don't even remember my head hitting the pillow.

I woke up to a knock on the door. I looked around in the near-dark room, trying to orient myself. I could hear one of the nurses say, "Clare...Clare, I need to talk to you."

I jumped up and fumbled in the dark toward the door. Approximately half an hour had passed and I had fallen into a deep sleep. Fear took my breath away as I observed the expression on the nurse's face. Before I could say or ask anything came the words that sent a jolt of fear through me. "Alicia appears to have taken a turn for the worse. We are getting ready to take her for a CT scan."

The nurse and I quickly made our way down the hall. Every step felt like a mile; as though we took forever to make our way down the short hallway. All I wanted was to see my girl. What was happening?

The nurse briefed me along the way. Alicia had woken up again with severe pain and vomiting. She showed signs of an increase in intracranial pressure.

As we entered the PICU, Alicia's bed was being quickly whisked down the hall toward the elevator. She was moaning, in and out of consciousness. "Mom, my head is killing me; it hurts so bad." I've been an ER nurse for many years, the fear I felt probably was not evident. I was trying to be there in each moment and reassure my scared and hurting daughter, who I loved more than life itself.

I walked with her, held her hand, helped when I could and listened to every word spoken. As a nurse and a mother I tried to make sense, of what exactly was going on.

Following the CT scan, we re-entered the PICU. As the nurse placed Alicia back on all the monitors and rechecked her vital signs, I noticed that Dr. Duncan arrived from home and was now present, along with the rest of the neurosurgical team. Although I was relieved that he was there, a new fear bloomed. Something was apparently going terribly wrong. They were all gathered around the CT scan viewing monitor, discussing the situation.

Dr. Duncan called me over to fill me in on the latest details. I let go of Alicia's hand and walked over to the area where they were standing. "There are some changes on Alicia's CT scan, but they may be typical after this type of surgery. There is no bleed. We are watching her changes very closely now and will be deciding if anything needs to be done as we move along."

I went back to her side and sat close, holding her hand. Her eyes were closed most of the time, but she would frequently moan in pain, with a grimace on her face. "Mom, am I okay? Is this normal? Mom, it hurts so bad!"

It was about 3:30 am, my fear was turning to panic. I glanced more frequently at Alicia and her cardiac monitor, at the increased intensity of the nurse's activity around her. Her heart rate was dropping rapidly.

The doctors approached the bedside. I was holding Alicia's hand as she opened her eyes, looked at me, and said, "Mom, I think something just exploded in my head." Her eyes closed. I looked up at the monitor and saw that her heart had stopped.

Where does your mind go when it can not make sense of what is happening? Mine searches inward for answers. How do you do what you know you can not do? I was frozen, afraid to let go of her hand, fearing it would be the last time I would touch her. I slowly backed away from Alicia's bed as the medical team moved in to initiate resuscitation.

Dr. Lister, the PICU attending physician that night, approached to tell me that I could stay with Alicia as the team worked on her. I looked again at the monitor, which showed Alicia's heart was in ventricular tachycardia (V tach), a rhythm that doesn't allow the heart to push blood out into the body, the vital organs and the brain.

I knew what was going on; I knew why. I understood what had happened in her brain that caused her heart to stop. I was sure that the bleeding inside her brain was creating enough pressure to push against the brain stem, the part of her brain that regulates heart rate and blood pressure and all other vital functions, to such an extent that it was severely damaged. *Herniation* is the term. The fact was that my sweet, beautiful, loving and intelligent sixteen-year-old daughter was now dying.

I don't know how to do this, was all I could think. *What am I supposed to do?* I walked around in circles in disbelief. Dr. Lister, one of the most compassionate men I have ever met, came over to me to catch my attention. He pulled my thoughts back toward what was going on. "Clare, is there anyone you want to call? You should call someone to come and be with you." I couldn't think. As I stared through everything and everyone, I could not put one solitary thought together. He led me to the phone and asked me whom I would like to call.

I needed to have someone there to help me decide what to do. Of course Paul would be called, but he needed to take care of Bryan and Crissy first. I definitely would call my parents, but because it was somewhere around 4 am I decided to wait.

Within a second I decided who would be the best to call and why: my younger sister Theresa, who was also a nurse. She lived in Litchfield, about an hour away. I knew that she would understand all that was going on and help me figure out what to do next.

Dr. Lister put the phone in front of me and entered a pass code so that I could call long distance. I couldn't dial the phone; I'd forgotten how. I had to think hard to locate her number in my memory, a number I usually dialed every day. After several attempts, I dialed and Theresa picked up. "Tree, Alicia just coded," I said. "I don't know what to do. She's dying." I heard her say, "Oh, my God" over and over. She was very upset. She may have asked me more questions, but I remember saying, "I don't know what to do." She said, "I'm on my way."

I returned to Alicia's bedside as the team worked on her. Dr. Duncan had drilled a burr hole through the top of her head and put a catheter into her brain in order to evaluate and relieve the pressure in her brain if necessary.

A normal pressure reading of the ICP, or intracranial pressure, is between 0 and 15. The doctor yelled out to the recording nurse that Alicia's opening pressure was 48. I knew that number was incompatible with life.

As the PICU team set the wheels in motion, Dr. Duncan came over and informed me that Alicia had bleeding inside her brain and that he was going to take her back to surgery.

I signed the permission forms. Alicia was prepared for transportation to the operating room. As I walked over to her, I was conscious that it might be the last time that I would see my girl, the one who I loved so much from the moment I laid eyes on her sixteen years ago. I held her hand as she lay unconscious. One tube emerged from her head; the tube from her mouth was connected to a ventilator that did all of her breathing, because her respiratory function had stopped. She also on monitors and had as many intravenous lines and pumps connected to her as I had ever seen in all my years of nursing.

None of this seemed real. I glanced around the room and then looked back at Alicia. Surely this could not be happening? How could this be happening? I remember holding my hands to my head and thinking, *I have no idea how to do this.*

Theresa arrived just as Alicia was being moved by her entourage down the hallway to the elevator. All that had just happened somehow hadn't really happened until I had to recount the details of the last hour or two out loud to my family when they arrived. Emotion started to overwhelm us; life was standing still. I became lost in thoughts and feelings. I was never in my life as much in the present moment as I was in those seconds, minutes and hours.

My beautiful girl was back in surgery. My only certainty was that her neurosurgeon was excellent and very fond of the inquisitive, funny and vibrant young lady he was now attempting to save.

Within a short time, my sisters, Paul and I were all in the PICU family waiting room. We alternated between pacing and sitting, rethinking every detail of what had happened up to that point. Around 5 am Theresa called my parents and they, as well as my brother Robert, arrived a short time later.

What seemed like forever, probably was only an hour or two before we saw Dr. Lister walking slowly down the corridor between the PICU and the waiting room. He came over and put his arm around my shoulder and said that Alicia had made it through the surgery. He told us that Dr. Duncan would be up to speak with us as soon as he could.

At about 7 am Dr. Duncan walked into the family room. He pulled off his OR cap, rubbed his head and started to describe the surgery and the events leading up to it. "Well, she's pulled through the surgery. We opened the surgical site. I took out a piece of bone that had been put back in place after the first surgery. There was a lot of blood in her brain. It looks as though a clot formed in the area of the first surgery, and the pressure behind it caused a bleed into her cerebellum. I had to take out a small section of her cerebellum." As if anticipating our questions, he interjected that it wouldn't be clear what deficits she would have because of that yet.

The major concern came next. "I also looked at the brain stem and could see that it has been significantly damaged. I'm not sure how she is going to do. I stopped the bleeding and cleaned out as much blood as I could, put the piece of bone back in place, and closed her up. Now we wait."

CHAPTER 5

Huddle Together and Stay Numb

TEARS ARE WORDS THAT
NEED TO BE WRITTEN.

~Paulo Coelho~

THERESA AND I WENT BACK IN TOGETHER to see Alicia. Her head was bandaged; the ICP catheter was still in place, protruding from the top of her head. Her eyes were closed. She was on a ventilator and an array of medications hung from several IV poles.

As we entered the room, her nurse first asked us how we were doing and then went on to explain which medications were infusing. She explained the details of Alicia's current condition and answered all of our questions. I noticed that Alicia's blood pressure was low and her intracranial pressure (ICP) was in the mid 20s. I kept looking over at Alicia while trying to hear and wrap my head around all the details being explained. She lay still, the ventilator delivering every breath for her. My sadness was overwhelming; my fear unspeakable.

Theresa and I stood there in silence, looking over the situation, shaking our heads in disbelief, our worst fears unable to pass our lips. We would be snapped out of this every few minutes or so by an alarm, the noise of the ventilator or the sound of one of the nurses talking. Little did we know we were doing just the right thing...taking one moment at a time.

Over the next hour or so things appeared to be heading in a bad direction yet again. Alicia's blood pressure continued to drop, as did her heart rate, and her ICP began to creep up.

At around 10 am, Dr. Duncan returned to the bedside to voice his concern that she might still be bleeding. He ordered another CT scan of her head. As the team quickly prepared Alicia for transport, they tried to deal with her worsening condition.

Theresa and I looked at each other in horror. Alicia's blood pressure dropped to the point that her nurse was unable to feel a pulse. Dr. Duncan decided to take her back to the operating room without doing the CT scan. She was too critical. Her body was once again shutting down.

Dr. Duncan rushed me out into the hallway at about 10:30 with a permission form that once again needed to be signed for the surgery. As he put the papers on the counter for my signature, the team rushed Alicia toward the elevator. Alarms sounded. Nurses, doctors and a respiratory therapist surrounded Alicia's bed; several were pushing IV poles that were infusing additional medications. Resuscitative measures were being carried out on my little girl while rushing her quickly down the hall.

Countless thoughts went through my head. What a horrific sight to witness! I was thinking all the time that this might be the last time that I would ever see her alive. Should I say good-bye?

Theresa and Dr. Lister were at my side; Theresa and I were in tears. Dr. Duncan explained what needed to be done. He lingered for maybe five seconds after I signed the form. I remember saying, "Don't worry about telling me anything more; please just go and save her."

He turned around with a look that I had not seen on his face before. "I will try everything I can," he said, "but you need to know—the situation is desperate. I do not expect her to make it." He turned and quickly walked away toward the elevator.

Dr. Lister was on one side of me and Theresa was on the other. We walked slowly toward the PICU waiting room, where the rest of my family was gathered.

Theresa and I exchanged glances, ones I will never forget. I stood still, not knowing what to do next. My feelings made it into words; while walking in circles, holding both hands to my head, I said, "I can't do this. I just don't know what to do. I can't believe it."

I turned to Dr. Lister and looked at him in desperation. In genuine search of an answer I asked him, "What are we supposed to do?" He put his arm around my shoulder, turned to walk with me down the hall to my family and friends gathered there and said with the most compassionate voice: "You huddle together and stay numb."

CHAPTER 6

The Rose

IN THE PRESENCE OF LOVE THERE ARE MIRACLES...
LIVE LOVE, GIVE LOVE AND MIRACLE
WILL FOLLOW MIRACLE AND WONDERS WILL NEVER CEASE.
~Deborah Brooks~

AT 11:00 A.M. THE SUN SHINING through the seventh floor windows filled the room, entirely unnoticed by anyone present that morning. Our closest friends and family had arrived and were sitting in any available space in the pediatric intensive care waiting room. We all were immersed in our own thoughts, intermittently disturbed by a few words of encouragement from any one of us gathered there. At that point the adrenaline was wearing off. It had been flowing through everyone's veins since they had been called in the wee hours of the morning with the shocking news that drew them all here to share in the unfolding events.

Occasionally an emotional discussion began. Tears flowed as someone expressed disbelief in what was happening. I remember being numb, staring off into space with no thoughts at all, only to be brought back to the terror by a stray thought, a momentary flashback to the terrifying circumstances of the past several hours. *How can this be happening? It was not supposed to; this can't be real.* I would sit for short periods and then spring up, as if the urge to escape the present reality was even a possibility.

Both of my parents and a couple of my closest friends, Marge and Ellen, sat together and quietly prayed. The familiar prayerfulness was an acceptable comfort— one, however, that I could not participate in at that point. My thoughts were a million miles away.

It felt almost as though I was watching an event unfold that we were all trapped in yet unable to do anything about, a true nightmare. We all searched for answers and then tried to find a way to deal with the reality. I distinctly remember thinking many times, *How do we do this?* The circumstance was totally foreign to all of us there that morning. There was lots of pacing, and the words "This can't be happening!" were muttered more than a few times.

I wondered how I would ever know how to deal with the very real possibility of my my loving, sweet, wonderful, first born daughter being taken from me...from all of us.

Just twenty-four hours earlier Alicia had run up the stairs prior to her surgery. I could still clearly picture the smile on her face as the elevator door opened onto the third floor the morning before. I closed my eyes tightly, full of sadness, in disbelief of what was happening.

Time stood still. Hours went by that might as well have been days. What do you say to God when you have exhausted every prayer and have pleaded, negotiated, bargained and begged "Please *no!*" I couldn't imagine going on without someone who I loved so very much, while at the same time being aware that her death was perhaps imminent. I tried to wrap every ounce of understanding that I had ever possessed around something that simply would not be understood.

More than a few times I recalled how terrified Alicia was of death, so much so that she would not even look as we passed a cemetery. Would she understand in her innocence, somewhere in whatever thoughts she might still be capable of, what was happening to her? How could I protect her from her ultimate fear? I thought about how there was nothing I could do; my helplessness was frightening. Terror was all I felt for her—for myself.

The world outside my thoughts slowly disappeared. I was hardly aware of what was going on in that room filled with the wonderful friends and family who would do anything for me and for my beautiful girl. I reclined on the couch everyone had left vacant for me. Chairs were placed around me, allowing me some space to be there alone with my thoughts, yet surrounded by love.

I thought through every alternative for what was happening, or could happen, considering how very damaged her brain was known to be. Would she survive, and for how long? If she did, what kind of life would she have? In one last pleading moment I assured God that if she lived, I would do anything. I hung onto Alicia in the depths of my heart and would not let her go. She couldn't go. I would do anything I could to save her, and as a mother, I believed I somehow had the power to do that.

Phone calls were made as we all sat together in utter disbelief, in absolute fear of what might lie ahead. My mother, a devout Irish Catholic woman, had not only been very involved in her own parish over the years but was also an active member of several groups whose only purpose was to pray for those in need. As we waited, a web of prayer that literally spanned the globe was set into motion.

When it comes to devout, caring, praying individuals, one thing is for sure—they have other friends who also pray. A single phone call will not stop with the individual at the other end of the phone; these people are serious about what they do. There are thousands, perhaps millions, of prayer groups around the world that are set up with the sole purpose of interceding with God for a particular intention or a person needing healing of body, mind or spirit.

On that particular morning in February, Heaven was stormed with requests to help keep one sixteen-year-old young lady in surgery at Yale New Haven Hospital alive. Miracles were asked for; love branched out around the world.

Our family is from Ireland, and we also have relatives in Australia, England, and Scotland, as well as here in the United States. Within an hour, one call after another was made; aunts, uncles and other family members were contacted, plus everyone they knew who possessed the ability and desire to pray.

Gradually the word of what was happening with Alicia got out to family and friends around the world. My younger sister is a Catholic nun. Her community, the Sisters of Mercy of Alma, as well as the churches they are involved in, both in the US and across the world, were notified of the need for intercession for Alicia. God only knows how many individuals, groups, men, women and children prayed that morning for the sweet young girl from Connecticut whose life was in danger.

I'm not sure if it was the prayers being said or a wisdom inside of me that I finally acknowledged; as the hours went by I had a moment of enlightenment. I realized I was powerless to help Alicia, and even though I would give my life for hers if given the choice, the charge of her life had been taken from me.

I became keenly aware that life might very well never offer her more than a vegetative state. Overwhelming sadness rushed into every cell of my body. My tears flowed. All of us there shared glances as we dealt with our own feelings and thoughts. I felt as though my heart was broken. Then in a second, I let go. I talked to God, to a power greater than myself, one I had always looked to for wisdom and truth and life, and said "Lord, I give Alicia to you. If it is better for her not to live, please take her."

I felt guilty for even thinking that. I wondered if I'd given up a fight that I still should be fighting for her. For some reason though, after making a conscious choice to give up control that I clearly didn't have anyway, a peace came over me that replaced the overwhelming fear and sadness. By all outward appearances all was not well, but a calmness had crept into my soul.

Alicia had always been a very religious girl. She played an active part in a thriving parish and at Catholic school. Most of her friends were also a part of and very active in our school and parish. Faith was a strong force in our lives.

Alicia had a special devotion for St. Therese, the Little Flower. My mother had taught my children about the lives of individuals who were holy and loving and strong, strengthened by their faith. It is said that those who share a devotion to St. Therese would be showered with roses as a sign of her interceding to God on their behalf.

Alicia had read the *St. Therese Prayer* countless times in her life.

> *O, Little Therese of the Child Jesus, Please pick for me a rose from the heavenly gardens and send it to me as a message of love.*
>
> *Oh, Little Flower of Jesus, ask God today to grant the favors I now place with confidence in your hands.*
>
> *St. Therese, help me to always believe as you did, in God's great love for me, so that I might imitate your "Little Way" each day. Amen*

Within approximately fifteen minutes of my relinquishing any control and placing Alicia in God's hands, a friend of Alicia's from school knocked on the door to the PICU waiting room. Someone got up and opened the door for her. She was a young lady who Alicia had become friends with during freshman year. One of Alicia's strengths was her unconditional love and acceptance for everyone she met; she easily befriended most of her school mates.

Ekta couldn't have possibly imagined what she would be walking into as she came to visit her friend; she was expecting to say hello and then to see her back in school within a couple of weeks. We gave a brief explanation of what was happening with as little emotion as we could. Tears rolled down Ekta's cheeks as she wished Alicia and us well. After we bid her farewell and thanked her for coming, she turned to leave the room. She took a few steps and turned around, as if she had almost forgotten;

she reached into her bag and said, "Could you please give this to Alicia?"

She placed one long-stem rose on the table with a card before she turned and slowly left the room.

At approximately one o'clock, Dr. Duncan made his way down the hall toward the PICU waiting room, a serious but relieved look on his face. He told us that Alicia had made it through surgery. There was a lot of bleeding, which he believed was now stopped. He had to take out more of her cerebellum, which was severely damaged by the bleeding and pressure. He reminded us again that she was very critical and that only time would tell the extent of the damage she had experienced.

CHAPTER 7

Life on the Seventh Floor

To live without hope,
is to cease to live.

~Fyodor Dostoevsky~

I HAVE THOUGHT OFTEN ABOUT THE circumstances that we faced during that difficult time and wondered how we were able to look past them to find hope in the midst of the most discouraging of situations.

By some sort of grace, some blessing, we were able to accept what was happening and, at the same time, balance that with the drive to carry on and to fight. Have you ever had the feeling that in the midst of all evidence to the contrary, when all the facts say you are wrong, deep in your heart you feel that you are right? At many points along the way, my sisters and mother and I would see some sign that Alicia had some kind of awareness; she would make the slightest movement or facial expression. These were usually not observed by any of the staff. When we mentioned what we had seen, we were not quite sure if they might have thought that we were wishfully imagining it.

Hope is an emotion that speaks loudly to those who are listening. It wasn't that we had stronger faith, or that we were geniuses. We certainly didn't know any of the answers about how to make Alicia better. All we did was wait with her and listen to our hearts.

The most difficult thing at that time was to quiet the fear and sadness in our hearts and be able to go on in a productive way. Through the amazing support of so many, our anxieties, heartaches and each of our personal fears were lessened. We were able to let go of unrealistic desires and any control we thought we had. No longer anxious with an end result in mind, we accepted small changes as they came and rejoiced.

Believing that miracles were possible, no matter how small, opened our eyes to the possibilities and brought us the strength to persevere. The support and encouragement we were given allowed us to pass hope on to Alicia.

The love of family surrounded us at every turn. My parents, the two sisters who lived close by, the other two who lived out of state, and my brother and his wife were either at our side or connected frequently to offer support or whatever assistance we needed. There was always someone there to get a hug from or give one to in those days. So many friends, ones we had already known as well as new ones, became pillars of strength that we could rely on as we held fast to a life that we no longer recognized.

Paul was able to take a week off from work during Alicia's first days in ICU; he sat in vigil at her side. He even became somewhat of an expert on the wave forms on the monitor, as well as the ventilator alarms, and he would alert the nurses if Alicia was in trouble.

My mother came to the hospital every day, not only to be there as a support and to do anything she could for Alicia, but also to take care of her own daughter. She would go to the cafeteria each day and bring me up something she knew I wouldn't refuse. She knew that I had taken eating off my list of priorities.

My younger sister Theresa also came in for hours every single day. She lived almost an hour away and had five children of her own. She was my partner in crime, as we brainstormed for ideas of concrete things we could do to improve the situation. We were willing to accept the things we could not change but, by God, if there was even the slightest thing that we could do to make a difference, we were all over it.

My dad had developed shingles in the early days of Alicia's hospitalization. I knew he was very frustrated about not being able to stop in and spend time with us at the hospital. However, he initiated a very efficient communication center. Anyone who called into the hospital trying to contact me was given his number. He received calls from many people every day and would relay messages and updates from us to those who stood by us on the outside.

Although many people wanted to come and visit us, my family discouraged them. No one was allowed in to see Alicia besides immediate family and an occasional close friend, who we would sneak in if the timing was right. If someone did come by, one of us would venture out for a couple of minutes to talk with them. My family was very protective of me and helped to maintain our privacy during that very difficult time. We were all very sad, scared, and exhausted, but we enjoyed some light and comforting moments with family and friends during Alicia's stay in the Pediatric ICU.

For the first few weeks in the PICU, Alicia was in a dark room. The idea was to eliminate as much sensory input as possible. Individuals with brain injuries are very sensitive to light and sound, and any stimulation to their senses can cause an increase in intracranial pressure. A dim light was on in the room, and otherwise only the lights from the monitors and ventilator were visible. It felt like a cave. The ventilator was the only sound that could be heard most of the time. An occasional monitor alarm would go off above our subdued voices as we quietly attended to our girl.

An MRI was performed within a few days of Alicia's massive stroke; it showed severe evolving damage to her cerebellum, which controls equilibrium and coordination. One-half to two-thirds of her cerebellum had been removed, and the remaining portion was infarcted, or dying. Multiple evolving infarcts in the brain stem were also evident.

As a nurse, I can assure you that was the most devastating news I could have heard. Damage that was already just this side of life threatening was getting worse. Alicia was already in a vegetative state. Where could we go from there? In tears, I approached her neurologist, Dr. Susan Levy, on the morning that the report was given to me and asked her if there was any hope. She agreed that it was an ominous finding, yet as a mother, I believe she knew the importance of allowing us to hold on to some hope. Very solemnly she said, "Continue doing what you are doing. Don't pay attention to the MRI results; keep your eyes on Alicia." From that day forward, we did nothing but that.

Each new day brought new insights and new ideas, as well as discussions between my sisters and mother and I on what very real things we could do to change the present situation and help Alicia.

Most people around us saw nothing but an unconscious young lady connected to a variety of monitors whose readings frequently suggested a body that was slipping away. They could not see the fight in her. Theresa and I were confident that she still possessed it, and we used it in any way we could to bring her back to us.

Another test done within the first week after the surgeries was an EEG, to identify the damaged areas in her brain through electric impulses sent out from the nerves in her brain. It also evaluated the function of her cerebrum, the thinking portion of the brain. The report showed a moderate amount of abnormality to a few areas, due to the pressure that caused her brain to move forward as well as downward inside of her skull in the first couple of days during the hemorrhaging. There was, however, some hope. Slow but fairly normal brain waves were interspersed through areas that were otherwise damaged.

The brain is the most pivotal organ to our existence, yet very fragile. We could see Alicia laying motionless before us and clinging to life. We knew that her brain stem, the bridge between the thinking brain and the spinal cord and ultimately the body, was very damaged. No one could tell us without a doubt that the situation was hopeless, so we refused to be discouraged.

Until then, resourcefulness had for me been a personality trait that had virtually gone untapped. But as they say, necessity is the mother of invention. That type of necessity finds you searching within, as well as all around you, to find ways to make things work. If a solution did in fact exist, and there were things that needed to be done, and we were going to do them.

I contacted my cousin Brendan within days of Alicia's injury. His career as a molecular geneticist had brought him into the field of scientific research. I asked him if he knew of any way that I might be able to find out the latest in treatments for children with brain injuries. He sent me the link for CenterWatch, a very comprehensive site that included all types of research studies being done around the world for a large variety of conditions.

A few studies involving brain injuries in children were being done in the United States at the time, and although not just right for us, gave us hope. New treatments were being found every day for a variety of conditions, including acquired brain injuries. At that point, I decided that if there was a shred of hope to be found in any study being done absolutely anywhere we, in fact, would find a way for it to become a reality. We never gave up hope; our search continued.

As we mulled over ways in which we might be able to connect with Alicia, we found that she had actually given us some clues in the past as to how we might try to make her better. She had told me on many occasions that one thing she truly loved about our family was the way my sisters and I could just sit for hours and talk and joke about almost anything. She absolutely loved to be part of any get-together where Theresa, Margaret, and I would hang out for extended periods of time and include her in the conversations.

So Theresa, Margaret, my mother and I would sit on opposite sides of her bed nearly every day and talk about all types of things. We included her in the conversations, recounting happy memories of the past or just laughing as we usually would during whatever conversation came up. What would have driven any man crazy—a group of women talking over one another, laughing and carrying on, several conversations going on at the same time— Alicia thrived on. Theresa, my mom and I sat with Alicia for hours, surrounding her with that familiar and enjoyable atmosphere. Our goal was to keep the environment positive and interact with her as much as possible.

At that point she was still critical, definitely not a candidate for physical therapy. She remained on a ventilator with a variety of medications and nutrition being pumped into her; she did not move at all. We worked around all of it, massaging and stretching every joint of her arms and legs, fingers and toes, to keep her joints in working order. Her joints and muscles would have tightened up had she been left to just lie there, making any possibility of normal function down the road completely out of the question.

With little reason whatsoever to be positive at the time, we just were, because that was all we knew how to do. Alicia, remained unconscious, her eyes closed most of the time. She needed the ventilator to assist her with every breath and showed minimal and intermittent evidence that her reflexes functioned. We held her hands, gave her foot massages, applied nail polish and decorative tattoos—all things that she loved. Everyday we played her music and turned on her favorite show, *Passions*. Our goal was that she would be surrounded by the familiar, positive things that she so enjoyed.

Because we were with her continuously, we were privy to the most subtle of changes. We knew what we knew in our hearts, and we carried on in hope, knowing that although what we noticed was not seen by everyone and perhaps believed by few, no one could persuade us otherwise.

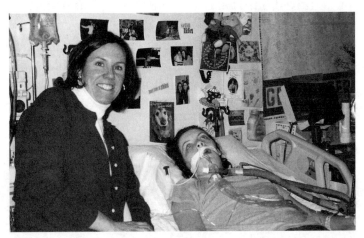

My sister Theresa and Alicia about 2 weeks after her third brain surgery

My mom visiting with Alicia in the Pediatric Intensive Care Unit

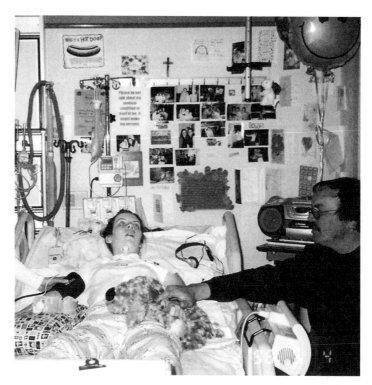

Paul and his girl.

CHAPTER 8

The Best of Care

THE WAIT IS LONG; MY DREAM
OF YOU DOES NOT END.

~Nuala O'Faolain~

ALICIA WAS CARED FOR DILIGENTLY AND profession-
ally by the staff in the Pediatric Intensive Care Unit
during her seven-week stay there. Bonds were established
from the very beginning when we met her caring,
knowledgeable and very down-to-earth and friendly
PICU staff. We had complete trust and admiration for Dr.
Duncan and his neurosurgery PA Eileen Ogle; Dr. Lister,
the director of the PICU; the neurologists Dr. Levy and
Dr. Testa; as well as the entire nursing staff. They spent
countless hours listening to us and addressing our every
care and concern. Their thoughtfulness, consideration
and respect for us as a family went a long way towards
helping us feel very comfortable. Right from the beginning, they kept us up to date on what was going on with
Alicia. They asked our opinions on a variety of issues, and
we were included in providing her care.

Theresa and I agreed that while the staff was amazing
in everything they did for Alicia and us, one thing was

missing. What they knew of Alicia was lying right there in front of them. She was motionless, almost lifeless. She could not communicate. None of them had known her before she arrived in the PICU on the fifteenth. At that point her progress was not at all encouraging. Although they provided the absolute best of care for her, they did not know who Alicia was.

Our goal became to show all of them who she was in any way we could, to say, "This is Alicia, and we are willing to do anything to get this girl back."

While always conscious that the nurses and hospital staff needed space and time to carry out tasks in the room, we did what we needed to do, respectfully and without getting in their way. Adequate wall space and tape made it all possible. I would venture to say that Yale's Pediatric ICU had rarely seen such a well-decorated, positive,and hopeful testament to any patient in their care.

Alicia had always been a photo bug. If she wasn't taking pictures of herself and her friends, she was thinking about what the next picture would be. When we put together a large collage of action pictures to display on her wall we had literally hundreds to choose from. They spanned the years chronologically and included family, friends, her favorite sports and causes and all manner of daring feats. In a day or two we transformed Room 1 of the Pediatric Intensive Care Unit, which could have felt like a sad and upsetting place, into a place where a special life was celebrated and displayed for all to see.

Alicia's high school, Holy Cross in Waterbury, had given us two huge, disturbingly yellow poster board cards containing the names of almost every student and teacher in the school-including notes, decorations and hand-drawn sketches to boot. When it was brought to us by one of Alicia's teachers, Theresa and I looked at each other and smirked. *Perfect!*

At every opportunity we would point out Alicia's passion for life, as shown in those pictures. The nurses, doctors, residents, respiratory therapists and everyone else who made their way into our home away from home gained respect for the hopes and dreams of the beautiful girl lying in front of them.

We also put a sign up that read: Please don't talk about my medical condition in front of me; it might scare me. We were very conscious of the possibility that Alicia could hear and comprehend everything that was going on around her; we thought it was very important to keep the atmosphere as positive as we could.

The first weeks in the Pediatric Intensive Care Unit brought Paul and I many sleepless nights. Alicia remained in critical condition and had experienced more than a few complications. Although any given day might present new problems, the nurses in the PICU developed a strict schedule. Each morning all the nurses, residents and specialists involved in Alicia's care met for morning rounds at about 8 am. I was allowed to participate in this process, because I was a nurse and very involved. I was allowed to listen in and contribute any ideas or observations that I had in regard to her care.

For the first weeks after the third surgery, specialists in many disciplines evaluated her function. Neurosurgeons, neurologists, ear, nose, and throat (ENT) doctors, speech pathologists, rheumatologists, immunologists, cardiologists, pulmonologists and gastroenterologists were all a part of her care and would contribute occasionally during the morning rounds. They all evaluated her and gave their impressions on her present level of functioning, as well as her prognosis. As her condition changed, adjustments were made to the course of treatment. She was monitored very closely by each specialist.

After I'd resided in the family sleep area in back of the PICU waiting room for about a week, one of the nurses brought up the idea of staying at the Ronald McDonald House, which was just a few blocks away. They thought that it would be a good idea for me to get some space and not be there all day, everyday.

The social worker made a call for me and set up a time to go and see it one afternoon. The Ronald McDonald House was a beautiful older home in New Haven. The thoughtfulness and care of the staff that I met during the visit was encouraging. The accommodations were beautiful, and since the house was lived in by parents and families of very sick children, they tended to every detail. Meals were prepared every day by volunteers, and snacks and leftovers were available to those who arrived after meal times. A pantry full of food awaited those who preferred to eat on their own at odd hours. Computers were available at all times, as well as free parking and all the love and support needed by families during their time of need.

My sister Mary from California was anxious to find a way to help. She and the Baudinet family, who were family friends, paid for my stay at the Ronald McDonald House in New Haven.

Each night I would call hospital security for a ride to the Ronald McDonald House, my new home away from home. This refreshing alternative to the way I had been living provided an oasis for me away from the hospital, even if only overnight. It was also convenient to walk a few blocks to the hospital each morning and be there in time for morning rounds.

About two weeks after Alicia was intubated, she started to breath on her own and no longer required the ventilator to take each breath. With that change, a decision needed to be made: Would Alicia continue to need the tube to keep her airway open? Even though she was breathing on her own, the tube prevented her from choking on saliva or other fluids in the back of her throat. Typically around the two-week period, a decision is made as to whether a tracheostomy tube needs to be placed in order to help maintain a patient's airway. Alicia was still unconscious. It was not yet clear if she would be able to cough or swallow in order avoid choking. We knew that her brain was very damaged but were not sure which of the cranial nerves had been harmed.

Twelve sets of cranial nerves emerge from the brain stem, one set on the right and one on the left. Each of them has a particular function in stimulating reflex-type responses from the neck up. They control motor functions involving the eyes, ears, vocal cords, epiglottis movement, swallowing function and gag reflex; these concerned us the most. We knew that multiple infarcts, areas of damage, in the brainstem almost guarantees that at least some of the nerves would not be functioning, but it wasn't clear which. There was only one way to find out. The doctor would take the tube out and see how Alicia would respond.

Alicia was evaluated by the ENT specialist and the gastroenterologist. The doctor put a thin fiber-optic tube down the back of her throat and visually assessed the area. Decreased function to the epiglottis and vocal cords was evident; each would, if working correctly, help Alicia maintain an open airway and not choke.

The plan was that the ENT doctor would take out the breathing tube the next morning. It would then be determined if Alicia would be able to keep her airway open. We would also learn if her cranial nerves were too damaged to assist her in swallowing or coughing, in order to keep her from choking.

If removing the tube worked, it would be a very happy day for all of us. If it didn't, she would be re-intubated and taken to surgery as soon as possible to have a tracheostomy put in. That would involve placing a tube through an opening in the base of her neck, allowing her to be suctioned, if necessary, in order to keep her airway clear. If the tube she now had in place remained any longer, permanent damage to the back of her throat, epiglottis and vocal cords would result.

On March 5 at 4 am, the tube feedings were turned off. The procedure was scheduled for 8 am, but after a bit of a delay- in the presence of the ENT doctor, anesthesiologist and several other medical personnel- Alicia was extubated at 11:50 am. Initially, she had a very hard time; her noisy respirations and grunts indicated swelling in the area of the epiglottis. The ENT doctor looked down her throat again with the fiber-optic tube and noted a lot of swelling to the epiglottis as well as dysfunctional vocal cords. She needed to be suctioned frequently, at least once every half an hour. Her cough was congested and very weak. She was watched closely throughout the day.

During the afternoon her friends Megan and Meaghan came to visit. Todd Dyer, Alicia's high school swim coach, came in around 8 pm and stayed till 9:30 or so. He read her stories, but she continued to have trouble breathing throughout the visit. She relaxed a bit as he sat next to her and read calmly. Finally, her eyes closed around 12:30 or so.

Alicia had a rough night with a lot of coughing and gagging, and frequently needed to be suctioned. This became worse around 5 am and by 6:30 her oxygen saturation levels were dropping. She opened her eyes to the sound of my voice, a scared look on her face. She gradually started showing signs of respiratory distress, sucking in air so hard that you could see her ribs with every breath. She was having a very rough time. Anesthesia was called; she was sedated and re-intubated at 7:20 am.

It was what it was, another discouraging day, another setback on the path to Alicia potentially bouncing back. That afternoon she was taken to surgery to have a tracheostomy tube placed. At the same time a gastrointestinal tube was put in, so that she could begin feedings and maintain her nutritional status. While these two interventions were necessary, we felt as though we had just taken a step or two back in the hope department.

As the weeks moved along, we all became familiar with the daily routine. A typical day in the PICU at that point began with morning rounds. I walked over each morning from the Ronald McDonald House to be there for eight o'clock. It was very comforting for me to be able to know exactly what was going on with Alicia and her care. The staff welcomed family participation in the process.

Theresa and my mom would arrive sometime in the morning for an update and then we would go and sit with Alicia. We gave each other breaks to go to the cafeteria or make phone calls, but we found it comforting to know that one of us would always be with her. We enjoyed each other's company as we always did; we held Alicia's hands, gave her foot massages, put on nail polish, or did her hair. They kept me updated on things going on out in the world, and we would just *be there* with each other. I can never in my life thank them enough for their constant support during the whole ordeal.

Paul had returned to work, but he came down almost every day, often bringing Bryan and Crissy. They received a lot of support from other family and friends, who had been driving them where they needed to be, having them over for supper or welcoming them to spend evenings with their families.

I realized Alicia's hospitalization was a very hard time for each of them; they went through their own struggles while their sister was so sick. Crissy was in eighth grade, and Bryan was a freshman in high school. There was no right way to soften these struggles; this was uncharted territory. We just did the best we could. Alicia was necessarily the priority and the focus of most of our attention.

During that time, families involved with the Watertown Age Group swim team that Alicia had so enjoyed being involved with the previous three or four years made and delivered meals to Paul, Bryan and Crissy daily for many weeks. That support and encouragement made a huge difference in helping us deal with the devastating situation we found ourselves in.

My dad continued to keep track of all that was being done, as well as all that people were doing in order to help us. A lot of visitors stopped in to offer their love and support on any given day. Chatting with friends as they arrived was such a relief; being able to let go of some of the emotion that at times felt overwhelming helped immensely.

Often in the late afternoons Alicia's friends stopped by to see her. Even though they tried to be upbeat, I'm sure the experience was horrible for them. Their dear friend, who was usually animated, funny and engaging, laid there motionless, expressionless and in critical condition. She was also hooked up to a variety of monitors and medical devices, appearing so different from the friend that they knew and loved.

Within days of the surgeries Alicia's teachers, guidance counselors and school administrators found ways to involve Alicia's friends, classmates and all the students at Holy Cross. Her friends and teachers banded together to do the one thing they could do for one of the people they very much cared for: they prayed. The chapel in the school was open throughout the day for her friends to support each other and pray for their friend. There were prayer assemblies every day for weeks. Students and staff sent out positive and loving thoughts with the intention to do whatever they could for Alicia. This was a powerful way to help those students who knew Alicia to better deal with the catastrophic circumstances.

In addition to Coach Dyer, one of her favorite teachers, Ann Estrada, also visited at least once or twice a week. They were both very supportive and spent many hours sitting with Alicia. They read books that they brought, as well as talked to her about anything that was going on at school that she might be interested in. Most of the time, Alicia's eyes were closed and she didn't move, so it was hard to know if she heard or understood what was going on around her. Yet they kept coming back and reading and hoping right along with us that Alicia would somehow bounce back and get well.

Right from the very beginning of Alicia's ordeal, one person after another—family, friends new and old, as well as groups of individuals—came forward and offered to help in whatever way they could.

Each day, my mom brought in cards that had been sent. The heartfelt messages of support and love absolutely elevated our spirits when we received them. So many people had already been doing so much to assist us in a variety of ways, but their conveyance of prayers and encouraging words went a long way during that time. There was a constant stream of information going back and forth between my family and all those who wished to do whatever they could.

The word had spread about what was happening with Alicia, as well as the fact that I was out of work indefinitely and staying near the hospital. People came out of the woodwork to do anything they could to contribute monetarily or with services.

Day after day, the cards kept coming in, sometimes with amazingly generous contributions. As we dealt with Alicia's hospitalization, day in and day out, that financial support was very helpful in making life easier.

While I was out of work my unit manager and coworkers called frequently to see how we were all doing, and friends would show up on occasion to take me out to lunch. One morning I drove up to Waterbury to speak with my unit manager, Robin, and the ER director, Dr. Jacoby. As I recounted stories of what had happened to that point, they couldn't have been more loving and thoughtful. Their support was very comforting, and they made it clear that I should do whatever I needed to do for Alicia. They were behind me 100 percent to take a family leave of absence. I planned to be out indefinitely and promised to keep them updated on Alicia's condition and progress.

A short time later, I was informed that a few of my best friends and fellow coworkers had received approval to start a fund in order to help me financially while I was out of work. Robin and my close friend Jane set up a program with the payroll department, wherein employees could contribute some of their paid time off into a fund set aside for me. I learned that Robin spent hours in the payroll department; Jane personally went to all the units in the hospital to explain my situation and asked everyone to help. Shortly thereafter, money was direct deposited into my account, which had been set up with my payroll deduction plan. I was paid for forty hours a week for over six months. I am forever grateful to all who helped us in such loving and thoughtful ways during that time.

There was also a huge fundraiser sponsored by the Holy Cross Father's Club, which organized and put on an amazing ziti dinner benefit and auction. The evening of the dinner I arrived from the hospital; as I walked down the hallway leading to the cafeteria, I noticed that the walls displayed many pictures of Alicia and her friends. It almost took my breath away.

This gathering was a very emotional night for all of Alicia's family and friends. For the first time since the ordeal started, there were opportunities for those present to share words of encouragement. Such an outpouring of love and support was amazing, and a bit overwhelming. *Eternally grateful* is a term that doesn't begin to describe how I felt about such loving kindness displayed by so many. I also appreciated that my sister Theresa offered to be the spokesperson for the family and thank everyone for coming. With my heart still so full of sadness, it was nearly impossible to express any of my feelings. Our family is forever grateful for the outpouring of love and all the work done that night.

I was humbled that people were giving so very much of their time, energy and money to carry us through that time. It boggled the mind.

On the evening of March 19, during a routine daily exam, one of the newer residents noticed that Alicia's pupils were unequal. They had never been quite right since her surgery. He contacted his senior resident, who then came and checked Alicia. Any change in Alicia's condition was reason for concern; I could feel myself moving closer to panic.

An MRI of her head was booked for the next day. We got the results later that day; they were not good. A collection of fluid called a subdural hygroma was building in the right side of Alicia's brain, a different area than affected by her hemorrhage on Feb. 16.

Anxious thoughts rushed in once again. Whether this new problem would worsen or delay any potential progress for Alicia was incredibly scary at that point. Dr. Duncan decided that they would wait until morning before making a decision about what to do. There was some discussion about whether or not to put a shunt in, which would drain excess fluid from her brain, but her doctors were concerned whether she was too fragile to undergo a major surgery yet. The next morning Dr. Duncan came in to tell us that he decided to simply put a drain in place for a day or two and then reevaluate.

On the morning of March 21 Alicia underwent yet another surgery to remove the fluid from the right side of her brain and put another temporary drain in place, which was removed within a week.

We then crossed our fingers and kept moving forward.

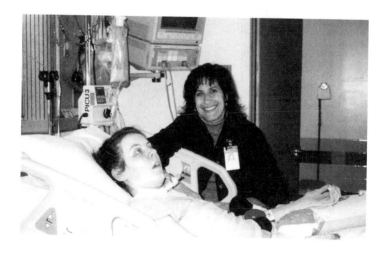

Alicia with her neurologist, Dr. Testa

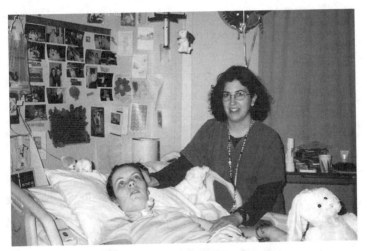

Alicia and one of her PICU nurses the day before leaving the Pediatric Intensive Care Unit

CHAPTER 9

Searching for the Next Step

CLOUDS COME FLOATING INTO MY LIFE,
NO LONGER TO CARRY RAIN OR USHER STORM,
BUT TO ADD COLOR TO MY SUNSET SKY.
~Rabindranath Tagore~

AS WE APPROACHED THE SEVENTH week in the PICU, considering that she had not had any discernible setback in over a week, the team decided to plan for Alicia's discharge from the hospital. Although in some ways that seemed like a welcome sign that progress was still being made, we were also faced with the stark reality that the Alicia we presently were focused on each day was certainly not the person who we had planned to leave with from the hospital.

We met with the discharge planner, anxious first of all to learn of our options. We were encouraged that there was hope Alicia would continue to progress. The planner pointed out immediately that she had met with Dr. Duncan and Eileen Ogle PA, as well as the speech and physical therapists who recently had been in to do their evaluations.

We had met with the speech therapist over the past couple of weeks to determine whether we could come up with some way to communicate with Alicia; at that point, it was all very one-sided. We were convinced that Alicia had done several things to indicate there was a link, no matter how thready, between her thinking brain and her ability to communicate. She would slightly wiggle her toes each time we put nail polish on her nails and the look in her eyes would seem a little brighter when we addressed her directly. We had not yet established any certain way for her to be able to make clear what she needed or had on her mind. We were so close, yet so very far.

We continued to wonder how much potential Alicia had to make further progress. Every time we asked Dr. Duncan or Dr. Levy, the answer was always, "We just don't know."

During the meeting, the discharge coordinator informed us that Alicia was not yet a candidate for an acute rehabilitation program; she had shown no signs of cognitive ability, and no one was quite convinced that the signs that we had seen as hopeful were more than reflexes. To hear that was very discouraging. The ground we were standing on seemed to waver under us.

Theresa and I inquired about what programs were available in the state that Alicia might fit into, considering her present situation. After discussing a few options for long-term care, she brought up the plan that she considered the best. We hung on every word as she described options that could offer a glimmer of hope for ongoing improvement for our girl.

We were leaning towards a sub-acute rehabilitation therapy program, and the Hospital for Special Care in New Britain was one for us to consider. She already had contacted an intake coordinator there and discussed

Alicia's case. The planner went on to say that because Alicia was not currently initiating any movement on her own, she would not be considered a candidate for the sub-acute rehab program yet. She suggested that she be placed in one of their affiliated convalescent homes, where her progress would be monitored for possible inclusion into their program in the future. Theresa and I looked at each other. Although the woman continued to speak, we knew the conversation was over.

We politely thanked her for presenting us with the options and for her time in making connections in Alicia's regard. We explained that we were going to have to talk further about the situation as a family. We asked how much time we had to consider the options. She said that we should try to come up with a decision within several days.

As soon as the woman was out of sight, we both looked at each other again and said almost simultaneously, "There's no way in hell she's going to a convalescent home." Once the shock wore off, we were both more committed than ever to figuring the future out for ourselves.

We decided that if Alicia was not a candidate for any rehabilitation program, we would bring her home. Theresa pledged that she and her husband Mike and five children would stand by me, Alicia and our family, doing whatever it took to help me take care of her. We decided that we would plant a hospital bed in the living room if we had to, vowing that we would make Alicia a part of everything that we all did in everyday life. We would never give up on her, and we would try as hard as we both could to make her life as happy as it possibly could be. We were adamant to do all that was necessary, but we decided to first look into all the alternative choices that offered what we needed.

Because our conversation with the discharge planner emphasized the need for a pediatric sub-acute rehab program, our goal remained finding one that would take her as she was right now and begin working with her immediately.

We got on the phone, branching out to all of our friends who knew anything at all about long-term, short-term, acute or sub-acute care. We investigated programs around the country, discussed and researched what she would need. We learned that her discharge diagnosis from Yale was "locked-in syndrome following a cerebellar hemorrhage and brain stem injury." We inquired some more, looked online and, in the spirit of staying open minded, even discussed the idea previously offered by the discharge coordinator. Once again, we decided to say no to that. We continued to search.

In two days we found the place that sounded like just the right fit: Blythedale Children's Hospital in Valhalla, New York. We discussed Alicia's situation with staff over the phone, they asked to meet us and discuss in person what they could offer Alicia.

Theresa and I made an appointment for two days later. We met with a very pleasant and encouraging social worker who assured us that Alicia would be a candidate for sub-acute rehab at their facility. She even pointed out that they had worked previously with children who had locked-in-syndrome. The wheels were set in motion.

CHAPTER 10

Easter 2002

A JOURNEY OF A THOUSAND MILES
MUST BEGIN WITH A SINGLE STEP.
~Lao Tsu~

WE BEGAN NOTICING SOME SUBTLE changes in Alicia's appearance. She seemed to be paying more attention. Her eyes were open most of the time and seemed increasingly bright, although she was unable to move them. Still, we felt a glow that could only be coming from the fighting spirit within her.

There was a small delay in getting a bed at Blythedale, which worked out fine as far as I was concerned. We would be nearby at Yale for the Easter holiday.

During Holy Week, the Christian observance of the week leading up to Easter, Christians commemorate many significant events. It is ultimately a time of contemplation, gratitude, love and hope, a time often shared with family and loved ones. Remaining in New Haven meant many of those closest to us could come and visit and catch up on any progress that Alicia was making. Right from the start, the support of our loved ones had been the driving force that made this scary and unfamiliar path bearable. We would have ample opportunities to relax and enjoy our family and friends once again. Although we were not sure at that point if Alicia was cognizant of what was going on around her, we were confident we could help her feel some joy. We surrounded her with humor, joy and loving kindness each and every day.

⚜

As I mentioned before, our parish was an active community. Many of us were involved in a variety of ministries, as well as with the grammar school. In our close community, many people were anxious to help in any way. Offering spiritual support was an important and appreciated contribution.

The two priests from our St. John parish, Father Cooney and Father Dan, had given us huge support. They each came down to Yale to visit at least once a week. Fr. Cooney had been the pastor for many years at that point and knew my three children well. His humor and unconditional care and acceptance of us and our children, with all the ups and downs families with children endure, fostered an easy and comfortable bond.

Fr. Dan had also become a strong leader of the parish and school community although he hadn't been there as long. We looked to him for support, direction and a humor that immediately endeared him to many of us. He was a great guy. Fr. Dan thought that it would be a good idea to have a mass said for Alicia on an evening during Holy Week.

In the days prior to the mass, we had become friendly with a family whose son was just admitted to Yale New Haven Children's Hospital. He was twenty-four and had cystic fibrosis since he was a child. The disease took a huge toll on his heart, as well as his lungs. He was in heart failure and was very sick when he was readmitted to the Pediatric ICU. He had been on a transplant list for years without a compatible donor having been found. His chances at that point were very bleak.

Parents of children in the intensive care unit had so much in common that we were able to talk about our stories, hopes and fears, even those hopes that would never be realized. His mom and I spoke several times over those days. Without saying so, we encouraged each other to continue to fight for our dreams, fight for our children. Sharing that level of unspeakable fear and immeasurable love for the critically ill young man and woman we loved so dearly had a huge effect on me, as well as with my new friend.

Our common faith gave us strength. We talked about how our faith, as if a living part of ourselves, was evolving each day we were faced with such sadness and need. As I left to go to mass that evening, I assured her that I would have Fr. Dan mention her son as in need of our prayers and intention.

On Tuesday evening I headed out to mass at St. John Church in Watertown. The church was filled with our friends and fellow parishioners. All of them had come to pray for Alicia and to offer their support by sharing this time and giving their love to us, her family.

Although amazingly emotional, the evening was beautiful. Fr. Dan celebrated a custom-tailored mass. I found the intensity of his homily thought-provoking and encouraging. He spoke of Alicia and made connections with Holy Week, pointing out how we all have times in our lives when we must "carry a cross." He eloquently stated that Alicia had said yes to the God she loved and tried to serve so well. There was not a dry eye in the church; we were all elevated by a perspective that did not mention fear, sorrow or despair; rather we were filled with hopefulness, acceptance of what is and the love of God and one another. It was a beautiful evening, dedicated to love and support for one another, especially for Alicia.

I returned to Yale that night and went into Alicia's room. It was dark, as it usually was at that hour. Her eyes were closed. Within me was a renewed determination to stand by my girl with love and hope. As I walked out into the hallway, I saw my new friend walking toward me. There was something different about her. Her eyes were alive with joy; a burden seemed lifted.

Her first words were, "You're not going to believe it." We both smiled. I was not sure what *it* was, but any thing to smile about was important in that setting. "They found a heart and lungs for Adam; the donor is totally compatible. It's unbelievable."

I'm not sure if we did on the outside, but we were jumping up and down on the inside.

As we spoke, staff was preparing to fly her son from Yale to a hospital in New York City, where they would perform the heart/lung transplant—his only chance of survival. We wished each other well, shared one last good-bye and off we both went to continue to love and do whatever we could for our children as long as they remained alive.

As we prepared to be discharged to Blythedale, Alicia was moved into Room 744 on 7 West. There was a whole different atmosphere there that was refreshing. The staff was also amazing and we grew fond of them immediately.

Each time we relocated to a new room or facility, we decorated immediately. It gave us something to do but also brightened the immediate space that we would spend so much time in. Alicia was a big decorator. As part of our plan to do all the things that she would enjoy, appreciate or want to have a part in, we just did it.

True to the spring and Easter theme, we put up a floral border and bought a few dozen plastic eggs, the ones that can be opened so you can put whatever you'd like inside. We all had become quite accustomed to just going with the flow. Although exhausted in so many ways, we always looked for opportunities to do something fun and creative.

On Saturday afternoon, the day before Easter, my sisters and I were sitting in Alicia's new room and talking as we frequently did about most things under the sun. Alicia's eyes were open; she stared straight ahead and didn't blink. We moved Alicia's head into whatever position was necessary so that she would at least appear to be able to see whatever we thought was interesting at the time. Granted, the poor girl was at our mercy as we adjusted her position. She may have much preferred to stare at the wall versus looking at whatever we found on television or an activity we thought she might like.

We tried to discover ways to find the link that was now missing between Alicia's possible thoughts and her expression of them, which is the consequence of locked-in syndrome. As they say, necessity is the mother of invention. On that Saturday afternoon the idea hit me. Perhaps we could show Alicia that she had the ability to do something. The premise of retraining individuals with brain injuries is to create new neural pathways that will carry out a function that a different part of the brain used to control. Alicia's injury involved the brain stem, the only pathway out of the brain. That was why she was unable to move any part of her body except for a very subtle movement at the tips of both index fingers, thought by her doctors to be reflexive movements.

The plastic eggs inspired me with an idea. We had some string in the room, for a reason that I can't even recall. I put one end of the string into half of an opened plastic egg; I snapped the other half into place. I moved an IV pole hanging from the ceiling to a spot near the end of the bed that Alicia would be able to see when her head was situated just right. Then I laced the string through the loop and brought the remainder of the string back down to the bed, close to Alicia's finger. I cut it to the right length and wrapped a loop around Alicia's index finger tip. We moved her head so that her eyes were aimed at the egg hanging from the pole.

I told Alicia what I was doing. With full knowledge that she might not be able to hear me, let alone see or have any understanding of what I was trying to do, I explained it all. "Okay, Alicia, I wrapped the string around your finger. It's connected up around the hanger and down to the Easter egg. I'm not sure you can see it." I asked her if she could. There was no response, no movement—nothing. "Okay, now watch the egg." Her head was pointed right at it. "When I move your finger up, the egg goes down, and when your finger goes back down, the egg goes up."

Nothing,

"Okay, let's keep doing this a bit. I know you can't move your whole finger, but let's just keep doing it." I moved her entire index finger up and then down, over and over and over again. Then I said, "Okay, can you try to do that yourself? It's going to be hard because your body isn't listening to your brain all that well." I did it a few more times, each time describing what I was doing. "Hey, Leesh, want to try it?"

And guess what ?

Oh yeah, she did it! The movement was very subtle at first, then a little more noticeable—all by herself. She remained expressionless, without any other movements. She didn't look any different than she had on any other day for the last couple of months, but she did it! She moved the egg every time we asked. We'd found a link between her brain and the outside. Let the games begin!

You can only imagine how fast we ran out to show her nurses, who were a very encouraging and down-to-earth bunch. They were ecstatic right along with us. Phone calls were made. We were on cloud nine. We called it "The Easter Miracle."

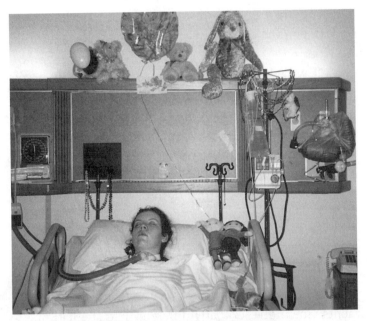

Easter 2002 – School Age Children's Unit
Yale New Haven's Children Hospital
(Notice the egg)

CHAPTER 11

Blythedale Children's Hospital

THE BEE DOES NOT FEAR ME,
FOR I KNOW THE BUTTERFLY.
~Emily Dickinson~

ON APRIL 1, 2002, ALICIA WAS discharged from Yale New Haven Children's Hospital. She was transported by ambulance to Blythedale Children's Hospital in Valhalla, New York. A new chapter in all of our lives was about to begin.

We were very happy with what we had seen when we'd toured the facility the week before. As we arrived for admission, our hopes were high. The fact that everyone we spoke with there felt that Alicia was nowhere near the end of the line in her ability to progress made us very happy. The hopeful, cheerful and warm atmosphere was inviting as well as reassuring. The facility was very clean. All the children we had seen appeared to be very well taken care of. Kids in wheelchairs were being pushed or making their own way around; children on stretchers came and went from therapies. The mood was joyful and bright.

Blythedale offered outpatient as well as inpatient programs and even provided a school in the building for kindergarten through twelfth grade. It was its own school district within the state of New York.

The inpatient area of the building had three sections: infants, school age and teenagers/young adults. A state-of-the-art therapy wing offered physical therapy, occupational therapy, speech therapy and an arts-and-crafts/recreation activity area where anyone could participate. The therapy programs were planned and implemented for any ability, even for minimally functioning kids. Other specialties were also involved, including a nutritional therapist. Alicia was evaluated by the doctor on her floor every day.

One thing that we found very reassuring was that Alicia was not the worst-off kid there. For some reason that made us very happy. We all hate to see anyone else having such difficulties in life but...well, you know. It's always nice to be on the "not doing so bad" end of the spectrum.

Within a very short time we were able to imagine a future that included dealing with a loved one with a profound disability. We learned slowly to accept and be comfortable with that. Alicia would be adjusting, working and making progress; so would we.

In the first couple of days there we were introduced to Alicia's therapists and teacher. She would be attending school while she was here. While they worked diligently to find a way for her to communicate she would be present in the classroom, allowed to absorb the information and activity going on there. At that point, she came and went on a stretcher, but she would be custom-fitted shortly for a new wheelchair.

Alicia still had a tracheostomy and was fed via the gastrointestial feeding tube (g-tube). She was nearly motionless, although she could move a couple of fingers. She was propped up so she was able to see and be part of what was going on around her.

Theresa and I were walking down the hall toward the cafeteria one afternoon while Alicia was resting. We were almost run over by two boys racing down the hall in their wheelchairs. We also watched a young quadriplegic woman in her mid-teens make her way to the therapy room by blowing into a straw to move her chair. Theresa and I looked at each other with smiles, knowing that we had made a wonderful find for getting Alicia to the best place for her. Her therapists, teacher, social worker, and physiatrist (a doctor who specializes in rehabilitation) were all very welcoming and excited to take care of Alicia. For now, we had found home.

The therapists worked with her daily, first in her room. Then they brought her to the large therapy room for access to more equipment. We were allowed to work closely with her care providers as they evaluated her needs and developed a plan of care for her.

Although she was still unable to move or speak, we observed a brightness in Alicia's eyes that we had not seen since she had her brain injury two months before.

We had been at Blythedale for less than a week before Alicia developed a fever. She had them frequently during her initial hospital course from infections in her brain, lungs and trachea, where the tube was located that assisted her in maintaining her airway. She was unable to swallow. As saliva was produced, it would just drain down the back of her throat into her trachea, to her lungs. She had developed a fever, as well as an increasing cough, and she had to be suctioned frequently. Her oxygen saturation counts were consistently lower than they had been.

Whenever an entirely immobile individual develops a fever, all possibilities are checked to find the cause of the infection. Urine and blood cultures and secretions from her tracheostomy were sent for evaluation. A chest X-ray was taken. A broad spectrum antibiotic was started, one generally prescribed to help fight a variety of possible bacteria, but after two days Alicia's symptoms had not subsided. Her fever continued. The decision was made to transport her back to Yale to investigate what was called a "fever of unknown origin."

Arriving back at Yale was painful in many ways, considering the gamut of emotions we'd experienced there within the past couple of months. However, familiarity brought a degree of comfort. I had the feeling that I would be able to relax just a little. It was a fever after all, not a life-threatening complication, as had occurred many times in the earlier days. After a round of IV antibiotics Alicia's infection came under control; we returned to Blythedale on April 11.

We started to notice some positive changes in Alicia's alertness and interactivity. She was even making progress in motor control. Communication was one of the priorities in those days. Her speech therapist worked diligently to establish a system that would allow Alicia to convey her needs, feelings and thoughts. A large selection of equipment in the assistive technology department was available to that end. The therapist constructed a variety of boards, at first with symbols and then letters, and worked on methods so Alicia could point at whichever symbol might express herself to the rest of the world.

Nothing seemed to be working. Though difficult and frustrating, Alicia's new level of attentiveness allowed us to explain what was going on and joke with her, tell her how much we loved her and convey a sense of hopefulness in the progress that she was making. While we weren't zooming in on exactly what was going on in her head, we were pleased.

The amazing therapists there had such positive, loving and caring attitudes. They instantly befriended Alicia, and I could see that their diligence was paying off. They worked through a variety of ways that she might appreciate and react to. Within a week or two of our Easter egg episode, Alicia was able to move her entire right arm and her head. It was hard to tell exactly what she did and did not understand, but she was certainly paying attention. I was able to be a part of her total care there; her slow but steady progress was a pleasure for me to see. We also tried to project forward and anticipate her becoming so much more functional. What a welcome change!

We celebrated Alicia's seventeenth birthday in the cafeteria at Blythedale and invited family and a lot of her friends, teachers and coaches to celebrate with us there. We were so excited about all of our friends seeing how far she had come. We thought it would be great to let her know how amazingly special she was to us by having a nice party for her on her special day.

We were not sure at the time what was happening, but on the day of her birthday Alicia was less responsive than she had been in a long time. Knowing that individuals with head injuries can be quite sensitive to overstimulation, we thought that might have been the cause. All of her friends gathered in the cafeteria and Mr. Killian, one of her teachers, brought his guitar and sang some popular songs. Alicia was actually shaky and appeared very out of sorts. She continuously bobbed her head back and forth, something that she had never done before. She seemed to be increasingly restless, so after forty-five minutes or so we brought Alicia back to her room. Everyone understood and was just happy to see Alicia and celebrate her special day with us.

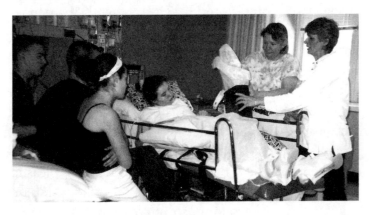

Celebrating Alicia's 17th Birthday with family and friends at Blythedale Children's Hospital

Exactly a week after her birthday party, on May 12th, I pointed out to the nurse that it seemed as though there were some spots in Alicia's right eye. I was concerned. Often she had trouble closing her eyes. Sometimes when she was turned over when her bed was changed or she was being washed, her face would end up in the pillow. I had seen the nurse's aids doing that in the past and had already mentioned my concern about it. I was sure that the spots in her eye were due to that when I mentioned it to her nurse again.

The next day I noticed that the spots seemed to be a little more pronounced; her eyes were tearing. I asked to speak with her physiatrist so that I could discuss this with her. She was not on that day. On Tuesday, May 14, Dr. Silverman sent us over to Westchester Medical Center Emergency Room to have Alicia's eyes evaluated. After a thorough eye exam, one of the ER residents voiced a concern that Alicia's optic discs, the part that can be seen near the retina, appeared to be bulging or swollen. She told me that was often a sign of intracranial pressure. I told her Alicia's full history and wondered if, following all the episodes of swelling over the last few months, it might be a lingering sign of increased pressure. She said that although possible, she could not be sure about that. She ordered a CT scan of Alicia's head to be safe. She also discovered that Alicia's corneas had abrasions, very likely caused by being turned onto her face when her eyes were open, as I had suspected.

The next day Alicia was to go to the ophthalmologist to have her eyes thoroughly examined. The resident said that the CT scan was abnormal; it would have to be compared with the previous one done at Yale. She would let us know about that at the doctor's tomorrow. We were sent back to Blythedale with Alicia on antibiotics.

The following day we returned to the Medical Center for the appointment with the ophthalmologist. The doctor said that Alicia's eyes would very likely heal well over the next week or two but wanted to speak with Dr. Duncan and have a copy of the CT scan sent to him for evaluation.

When we arrived back at Blythedale, Dr. Silverman put a call in to Dr. Duncan. The CT scan had been read as acute hydrocephalus with a large midline shift. The damage done by her brain injury was now blocking the normal flow of the fluid that circulates in the brain. Alicia was again accumulating a large amount of fluid in her ventricles, causing her brain to be pushed to the opposite side of her skull.

This was a very concerning finding. Dr. Duncan wanted Alicia back at Yale ASAP to have a shunt put in. A tube would be placed into the ventricle in her brain to allow accumulated cerebrospinal fluid to drain and prevent additional pressure inside her skull.

An ambulance was called for an emergency transport between Blythedale and Yale. However, Alicia's medical insurance in Connecticut would not cover an emergency ride from New York to Connecticut. It seemed ridiculous. We inquired about the cost to transport her, and the ambulance company said that it still would not be able to be done due to their regulations. A routine transport would possibly be covered, but transportation was not able to be done that day. If it was an emergency call, they would not be able to transport to a hospital in Connecticut. We made a few phone calls to verify this and, yes, in fact, it was the policy. We called AMR in

Connecticut, the ambulance company affiliated with Yale, but they were also unable to do the transport.

Our anxiety was already high, and now we were unable to get Alicia back to her doctor for emergency surgery. Panic set in. Dr. Duncan's PA, Eileen, called back to inquire about when we would be heading that way. At that point, we were trying to figure out if there was any way that we could transport her ourselves, even though we knew that was a bad idea. Then it hit me—I knew some people!

I called Robin, my head nurse at St. Mary's Hospital in Waterbury where I worked, and asked for another nurse's home number. Paula, who I had worked with for years, was married to Bill Campion, owner of Campion Ambulance Service in Waterbury. Within minutes the supervisor at Campion's called me back, and I told him our situation. We had no problem paying for the ambulance; however, everyone connected with Blythedale and Yale had just refused to transport Alicia for one reason or another. The supervisor told me he would call me back in a few minutes. Five to ten minutes later I got a call from him. A car with a paramedic was on its way, with an ETA of about an hour. I couldn't believe it. I'm not sure if Campion was reimbursed for the ride by our insurance; we never received a bill. I can't thank Bill and the Campion crew that transported us back to Yale enough. They are the best!

We left Blythedale Children's Hospital in a hurry and never said good-bye. We didn't realize at the time that we would never return.

CHAPTER 12

A New Beginning

TRUE LIFE IS LIVED
WHEN TINY CHANGES OCCUR.

~Leo Tolstoy~

WE ARRIVED BACK AT YALE FOR the third time just before 11 pm on May 16. My mother and Theresa were already there to meet us. Alicia was immediately examined by the neurosurgery residents, and although we brought a copy of the most recent CT scan, another scan was done to see if there was any increase in the size of the ventricles. Alicia appeared stable but was perhaps a bit less responsive than she had been on her good days.

She was admitted to the PICU. Dr. Duncan would be in to see us in the morning. Alicia was settled, and all seemed well. After making a phone call to inform Paul of what was going on, I went to sleep in the family room in the back of the waiting area. He would be down first thing in the morning.

Dr. Duncan was in early and went over the CT scan results with me. He decided to observe her and have a couple of other tests done. Alicia would probably have surgery on Saturday. Once again uneasiness crept into our hearts. Would everything go as planned? She had been doing so well and making progress. How much of a setback would another surgery bring? We were all quite tense, but this time we knew how to rely on each other, and that support helped us make it through the wait.

On Saturday morning my family arrived to wait with us as Alicia went off to surgery once more. Dr. Duncan met us before surgery and assured us that this was a routine surgery and he didn't anticipate any problems.

Following the surgery, as Dr. Duncan walked down the hall toward us I think we all stood up at the same time. Have you ever tried to figure out someone's facial expression from twenty feet away, before you actually talk to them, when you are anxious to get a feel for what happened? Well, that was exactly what I tried to do as Dr. Duncan approached. He walked through the door shaking his head. With a bit of a smirk, he said, "Well, she scared the hell out of us again!"

He explained that she had some type of reaction, and he admitted that he had no idea to what. He said as they were doing the surgery her hands and face started to swell right up, her oxygen level dropped, and they had a hard time ventilating her and getting the oxygen level up again. He said that the episode let up just as fast as it came on, but shaking his head, he lightly said, "Well, she gave us all quite a scare," to which I replied, "That apparently has become part of her charm."

She ended up in the ICU for two days because of some changes in her pupils' size and reactions. She became a bit restless during the night on Saturday and was placed back on the ventilator for a short period. Things quieted down over the weekend. She would be stable enough to leave the ICU for the regular pediatric surgical floor on Monday.

When Alicia was in Blythedale I had made a commitment to chaperone the 8th grade field trip with Crissy on Monday the twentieth. I was a bit anxious about going, considering Alicia was back in the ICU.

Many of my coworkers and friends had sent cards and let me know that they would be more than willing to help me in any way they could while Alicia was in the hospital. I made a couple of phone calls to see if anyone might be free on that Monday to sit with Alicia for a couple of hours. Two of my friends, Jan Hauck and Deb Blazys, both ER nurses, volunteered immediately. They came down to Yale and sat with Alicia all day while I went on the trip with Crissy. It was unbelievable how thoughtful and caring everyone we knew was during that time, so very often lifting huge burdens from our shoulders.

Alicia started showing dramatic changes in her level of functioning almost immediately after the shunt was put in. During the past month or more we had been trying various methods to communicate with her. Tuesday morning, Alicia was looking so alert that I gave it a go. I asked her if we should try to see if we could talk again. She blinked.

Hmm... "Hey, Leesh, can you blink again?" She did. I paused. "And again?" and she did. Has the thought ever crossed your mind when you weren't quite sure whether you actually saw something, *Hmm, did that actually happen?* Well, let me assure you that was the thought going in my head at that moment.

"Okay, Leesh, let's try something." Her face brightened up. "Leeshy, let me have you blink once for yes and twice for no, okay?" She blinked... Picture my huge smile. I added the moment to the list of the happiest moments of my life!

Within an hour we figured out a way to talk to each other. First I ran out to the nurses' station for a pile of paper, and then rummaged around for a pen.

I said, "Okay, we can go through the alphabet. You can blink when I get to the letter, okay?" Blink! I then began to ask her if a letter was a vowel (pause) or consonant (pause), and she would blink for one or the other. Then I would go down the list. I liked vowels the best! We took a few minutes to figure the system out...and then we were off!

"What's your name?" A- l - i - c - i -a

"What's mine?" M - o - m

"How are you feeling?" O-k-a-y

"Just okay?" One blink

"Do you have pain?" One blink

"Where?" M..y... h...e...a...d

 "Your head?"

At long last we were communicating. I couldn't believe it. The process was a bit drawn out, but we were getting it done. By the way, her head was hurting only on the outside where the incision was, not inside. Okay—whew!

I asked her, "Do you have anything you want to ask or tell me?"

She spelled out, "When am I going to wake up?"

I felt like crying for her. My poor girl didn't know that she had actually made it back into the living, wakeful world yet.

A thousand thoughts and questions filled my mind. I told her that she was awake now. I asked her if she knew what the date was, and she blinked out, "I don't know, February 20 or something??" I told her the date was May 21. I said that it was a long story, which I would tell her all about, and I assured her that she was awake and everythings was going to be okay.

We talked on and on into the evening. I rejoiced from the bottom of my heart. My girl was back—my girl was back!

Needless to say, the news circulated very quickly. Staff came in to see, with everyone as ecstatic as we were. Alicia's face was more expressive, right down to rolling her eyes, and she shrugged her shoulders to add to the conversations.

As the week progressed we both became very quick at asking and answering questions. She also started making strides with movement. On Tuesday evening she moved her left arm for the first time. She kept trying to see what she could do, starting with bending her elbow slightly and then lifting her arm. It was amazing, as though everything had just woken up. Each time she tried something new she was so excited. She was only able to move her left side at that point, but she continuously pushed herself to do more and more.

The speech pathologist practically made a beeline to our room to see what was going on with the girl of whom they had said just a month or so earlier, "There's nothing going on here."

Physical therapy and occupational therapy staff came in to do evaluations. I have never seen so many looks of absolute shock in my life as I did in the first days that Alicia started to show everyone what she could now do.

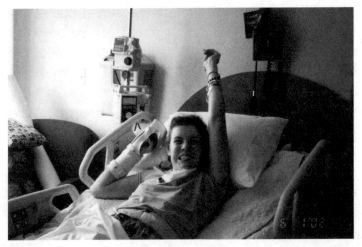

May 22, 2002 - Alicia showing off !

CHAPTER 13

Gaylord

COURAGE DOES NOT ALWAYS ROAR.
SOMETIMES COURAGE IS A LITTLE VOICE AT
THE END OF THE DAY THAT SAYS,
"I'LL TRY AGAIN TOMORROW."
~Mary Anne Radmacher~

FINALLY, THE DAY WE HAD ALL been waiting for arrived. On the morning of May 31, 2002, we gathered our things and prepared for a trip on the next phase of our journey. All the arrangements had been made.

As we said our last good-byes to the wonderful staff at Yale New Haven Children's Hospital, we beamed inside with joy at the possibilities that lay ahead. Three and a half months after we had arrived there on that cold morning in February, Alicia was finally able to feel the warmth of the sun on her face.

One of her favorite nurses, Michal, accompanied Alicia on the transport to Gaylord Rehabilitation Hospital in Wallingford. Gaylord hasa reputation for excellence in rehabilitation services for decades. Its specialties include aggressive rehab for individuals with brain and spinal cord injuries, as well as those who have strokes and severe pulmonary illnesses.

As Theresa, my mother and I drove up to Gaylord, we shared the joy, support and encouragement we had come to cherish so much over the past months. We had been through so much together. Our anxiety now turned to excitement, our fears transformed into renewed hope. Anticipation of the possibilities to be found on the road ahead wiped our sadness away.

We could never undo what had happened, but we were now able to look ahead. The nearly constant worry over whether or not Alicia was going to make it was finally quieting inside each of us. We had just landed on solid ground, and the feeling was wonderful. Faith held us together; hope carried us; love strengthened us and brought us to this day.

We arrived around noontime at the building where the atmosphere was full of care, joy and hope. Everyone we met was friendly and put us at ease immediately, conveying heartfelt welcomes. Everywhere we looked there was constant activity with patients coming and going, as well as staff interacting with patients and one another. We felt very comfortable .

We were brought to a room on Hooker II, the floor where individuals with brain injuries resided. Alicia was transferred from the hospital stretcher to a bed in a room that was to be her home for the next couple of months. The room was stark but comfortable. The nurses and floor staff set us immediately at ease. We said our last good-byes to Michele, who had taken wonderful care of Alicia on and off for many months.

Alicia was at that point participating in conversation mostly with body language, nods and facial expressions.

The valve in place over her tracheostomy allowed her to speak. However, her voice was almost inaudible and barely understandable after months of disuse. Not only was she adapting to speaking again with the trach, but she needed just the right amount of air to flow through her vocal cords in order to make a sound. Some damage had resulted in a degree of vocal cord dysfunction.

However, Alicia had no trouble communicating her needs. We still used our alphabet system when necessary, which was working quite smoothly.

Our first day at Gaylord was truly a joy-filled beginning to a new phase in all of our lives. Over the next couple of days we were introduced to all manner of staff who would be working with Alicia on a daily basis. She had evaluations by a doctor specializing in rehabilitative care, nurses, physical therapists, occupational therapists, speech pathologists, recreational therapists... Alicia was in the best of hands.

Theresa, my mom and I then did what we did best; we stood vigilantly in support of our wonderful girl. We observed all that was being done, learned how to help—and, oh yeah, we decorated.

With the permission and encouragement of the staff we transformed an otherwise bland and institutional-looking room into a home away from home. Decorations, borders, flowers, pictures and knickknacks from home, all the usual suspects, changed Alicia's room to a place of joy and warmth.

Alicia was very quickly custom-fitted with a wheel-chair, one that would deal with all of her limitations. She continued to need total support; she still had little strength. Her head and arms needed to be supported to stay upright and in a functional position. A tray was attached in front to be used for many of the therapies that she would need. The goal of being able to carry out the activities of daily living was a main focus of all her therapies; her chair assisted her in doing so.

Her new wheels addressed the physical aspects of Alicia's limitations. In a semi-reclined position in the chair her legs were well supported. Her circulation was poor due to a decrease in muscle tone from lying in bed for the past four months. The injury to her brain stem also meant her blood vessels weren't able to constrict and dilate in order to prevent clot formation; her reclined position helped offset problems in that area. At that point, coordinating movements of her arms presented a problem. She was always transported with the assistance of another person, but she was mobile, and that was a welcome improvement.

Alicia started each day at about 7:30. A physical therapy aide came to her room to do range-of-motion exercises. Compared to the more basic stretching of muscles that we had been doing with her over the past months, this new drill was a range-of-motion-on-steroids program. After a g-tube feeding for "breakfast," Alicia was given a shower. Either the occupational therapist or nurse would come help her work on dressing herself. Then it was off to a day of therapy.

Every day she went from occupational therapy to physical therapy to speech therapy, for an hour each. In her off time she was taken to recreation. A teacher worked with her in math and English. The teaching department was in contact with Holy Cross and coordinated which courses would be best to continue at Gaylord. The custom-designed, around-the-clock, intensive therapy program produced dramatic results within a very short period of time. It was nice to finally feel safe; the ground beneath our feet seemed solid at long last. A new hope was blossoming inside of us all. I distinctly felt as though we were out of the woods, although I was almost afraid to acknowledge my relief.

Alicia was healthy and progressing dramatically well. She finally was starting to be able to do some of the things that she enjoyed. She still had significant fine-motor coordination limitations and so was unable to write, but she was figuring out how to type again; that was huge. She was once again able to communicate with her friends and express herself. Her verbal communication was improving but still a challenge.

Although Alicia was making consistent progress, I decided to continue to stay with her when Alicia asked if I could. The staff had no problem with that arrangement at all, since Alicia was a child with communication limitations. We were grateful that parents were allowed to stay. She was the youngest patient on the floor at that time and got a lot of special attention from the staff, at least in part because of her pleasant disposition and witty personality.

I stayed in the room with her, which gave us a lot of quality time throughout the day and especially in the evenings. We would talk for hours about what had happened as well as discuss the possibilities for the future, considering all the changes that had taken place in her life. What a huge thrill to be able to communicate after going so long without it.

Friends visited more frequently and we would participate in a variety of activities on any given evening. Alicia enjoyed exploring the other areas of the building in our free time. We went to movies after dinner in the recreation room. We religiously watched a show that was on at ten o'clock, *Who's Line Is It Anyway?*, each night before we turned out the light.

The therapists at Gaylord geared their plans toward having Alicia carry out tasks that she previously had the ability to do. Each day she would try in a variety of ways to strengthen muscles and retrain the pathways in her brain that would allow her to move her arms and legs again. Part of the process involved repetitive motions in order to trigger muscle memory or make new pathways.

Alicia became very fond of all of her therapists at Gaylord; they went above and beyond to encourage her and help her regain her abilities. We felt so very fortunate to be working with such a professional and enjoyable staff.

One activity that Alicia enjoyed and excelled at was swimming. There was a pool at Gaylord, but there was one complication. Alicia still had a tracheostomy. The rule was that no one with a tracheostomy could be in the pool for a variety of reasons. However, since Alicia had been a very good swimmer and would benefit from and enjoy getting into the pool, her physical therapist asked for a special exception to the general rule. We bought a special waterproof-barrier patch to place over her trach and g-tube. She started having a few sessions of pool therapy per week.

It was a very thoughtful move on the part of her therapists. This privilege also put Alicia among very elite company. We were told that the only other person to be allowed in that pool with a tracheostomy besides Alicia had been Christopher Reeve some years before.

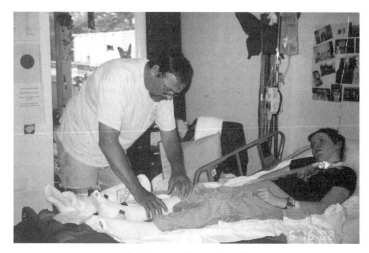

Paul adjusting Alicia's leg splints

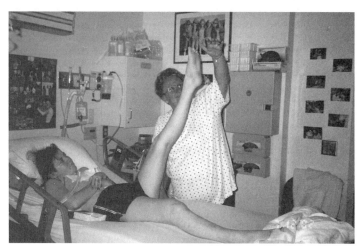

Morning stretching at Gaylord

CHAPTER 14

Going Home

HEAD UP, HEART OPEN...TO BETTER DAYS!
~T.F. Hodge~

ALTHOUGH WE HAD ALL ANTICIPATED and looked forward to going home, it was not as simple as we might have thought to walk in the door together and get on with life. When life as you know it has changed, will anything ever be the same? Not so much, we discovered.

Alicia and I had left our home on a cold winter morning six months before, leaving behind life as we knew it. I had by then come to accept our new reality; I'd learned to let go of what that previous life had offered. We had to appreciate what we still had and be grateful for all that we had received. Our lives were redefined by events beyond our control. Nothing would ever be the same, but Alicia persevered with extraordinary patience and acceptance of the situation.

While there had been much sadness, worry and pain in the new reality, the support and love of our family and friends had also brought untold amounts of joy, comfort and happiness. Our transformed world was not better, not worse, but changed. We now looked at life through

119

different eyes, our vision of the world and our dreams refocused.

Since peace would never be found dwelling in the past, we all moved on—cautiously at first, but then with the increased confidence that only comes from being challenged by adversity. Each day was a new day to be lived, one foot in front of the other..

<hr />

It was clear we needed to make our home more accessible for Alicia, at least the part of the house where she would be spending the most time in. Resources fell in our laps, one after another. There was time before we left Gaylord to prepare the house in a way that would accommodate Alicia's present needs. A discharge planning nurse from Gaylord came out to the house to help us think about what all of our needs may be and offer ideas for ways to make things more convenient and efficient.

Lots of equipment had to be either purchased or rented, including a hospital bed, commode, suction machine, oxygen saturation machine and suction catheters, oxygen tank, g-tube equipment, feeding pump and supplies, and tracheostomy supplies. We also needed linens, towels, bed pans, a recliner, and on and on—everything a well-stocked hospital room required, and more. We contacted the companies we would be getting the supplies from, and we were almost ready. All we needed was our girl.

At Yale we were given a head start on dealing with the financial realities that needed to be considered in regard to her medical expenses. While Alicia was covered by my insurance through work, many services would either not be covered or be fully covered only for a short period of time. The different outpatient therapies provided at Gaylord fell into that category. Luckily, many months before, a social worker at Yale had made out all the paperwork to initiate and apply for state insurance for the disabled, in anticipation of needs for inpatient and outpatient rehab programs for Alicia down the road.

After Alicia arrived home, she continued therapies on an outpatient basis two to three times a week at Gaylord Hospital. She made progress and regained strength and coordination, renewing her hopes of regaining lost abilities.

I was able to assist Alicia with her everyday needs. Being a nurse came in handy; we dealt on a daily basis with g-tube feedings, tracheostomy care and mobility issues.

When the three kids were back under the same roof there was such joy in the air. Bryan and Crissy helped in any way they could with Alicia's care, but they were exceptional in encouraging and sharing joy-filled moments with Alicia whenever they could. Wow ... had we missed our girl! We were ecstatic that she finally made her way back to us.

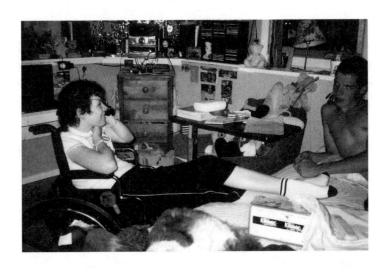

Back Home !!

CHAPTER 15

Feeling the Love!

Never believe that a few caring people
can't change the world.
For indeed, that is all who ever have.
~Margaret Meade~

WE WERE JUST BEGINNING TO reorganize our lives; we were still in a bit of a fog. Life went on and we kept moving, although sometimes it felt like we were not yet quite on solid ground. As I think back, I know that our amazing friends and family carried us through that time. We appreciated their amazing generosity and support at every turn.

Shortly after Alicia arrived home from the hospital in August 2002, a group of runners planned a fundraiser to benefit Alicia. My sisters Theresa and Margaret were members of a newly formed group, the Village Striders, whose main focus was to reach out in love and do whatever they could for anyone in need; the Striders also liked to run. The group had fourteen members at that point. I doubt a nicer group exists; they expend a lot of energy to allow others to "feel the love."

Naturally, Theresa and Margaret had told the members of the group Alicia's story. They knew of her remarkable progress; they admired her fighting spirit. With the intention of helping Alicia do or buy whatever she needed to realize her dream, they got together and planned their first fundraiser, to be held in September 2002.

They decided to enter the "Reach the Beach" relay in New Hampshire, a two-hundred-mile relay race from the mountains to the ocean at Hampton Beach, billed as the longest relay race in the country and held each year in September. Groups from around the country take part. Many groups use the relay as a way to raise money for a variety of causes. We were deeply surprised and excited when we learned that the Village Striders decided to make Alicia the focus of the "Reach the beach" fundraising effort. They did this by hosting a wine-tasting social a few weeks prior to the race that included pledging for miles run, a silent auction and general ticket sales.

We were astounded that this wonderful group of individuals was aiming such support and love toward Alicia and our family. Not only were they raising money, they were genuinely interested, encouraging and supportive. All the members of the Striders spent time talking with and getting to know Alicia and were excited along with her as she told them of her continued progress and dreams.

The wine-tasting fundraiser was a wonderful evening shared with many new friends, most of whom we continue to be close with to this day. The Striders have reached out each year to make the world a better place, and each year Alicia has been one of the benefit's recipients.

Village Striders at the Reach the Beach Relay
Hampton Beach – September 2002

Through bonds born of love and strengthened by friendship and the willingness to give unceasingly, as well as to receive when the situation presented, this wonderful group has grown to more than fifty since then. They share and celebrate each others' lives, as well as the gifts that they possess, frequently and with passion.

Alicia also was showered with another staggering demonstration of generosity. A group of friends, parishioners and other Watertown residents, some of whom we didn't even know at the time, got together and planned a series of fundraisers. They intended to help us pay for medical bills, as well as the cost of modifications that made our home handicapped accessible for Alicia.

One of the fundraisers sponsored by a variety of local groups was called Alicia Townsend Day, held at Veteran's Memorial Park on September 29. Alicia Townsend Day was a day where a community came together with the sole intention of generously showing love to a member of the community whose life had met with unfortunate circumstances.

The Girl Scouts, Boy Scouts, sports teams from Watertown High School, St. John Church Youth Group, the Lion's Club,and the local chapter of UNICO were all involved in making the day a huge success. The event raised enough money to remodel the downstairs of our house, enabling us to accommodate all of Alicia's needs.

In charge of the remodeling was our good friend Dennis O'Sullivan, who became the head engineer on the job, thinking through the details with exceptional care. Handicapped access to the house was an essential part of the remodeling. We also converted the garage bay closest to the ground level bedroom into an amazing, accessible state-of-the-art bathroom, complete with a roll in shower.

The whole job was absolutely amazing. Many individuals and companies volunteered their time, energy and equipment to make this huge project unfold.

Another fundraiser followed in the early part of 2003, raffling off a car. This fundraiser was also a huge success; the funds supplemented what had been raised already and allowed the continued renovations on our house.

So much love was graciously given by so many, all for the benefit of one young girl. Our family will forever hold an abundance of love and gratitude for everyone involved in these projects, and for the love that was lavished upon us during that time.

CHAPTER 16

The Christmas Road Trip

LIFE IS A CHALLENGE,

MEET IT.

~*Mother Theresa*~

ALICIA CONTINUED TO MAKE PROGRESS with her out-patient therapies in all areas except one.

In physical therapy, she strengthened her muscles and even made progress with her equilibrium while walking the parallel bars. She still was unsteady but continued to make strides.

Occupational therapy produced discernible differences as time went on. Although Alicia had problems with her fine motor coordination, which affected her ability to write, she continued to practice and gained more strength and coordination all the time. She was able to communicate through typing.

Alicia still couldn't eat, though not for lack of trying. While in Gaylord, she had started very early with the speech therapists to work on initiating nerve stimulation in the back of her throat and did every exercise possible with the goal of doing one simple thing: to swallow. That remaining brick wall was very discouraging and frustrating. She longed to be able to simply eat again. At one point Alicia remarked, "Sometimes I wish I hadn't lived. I wouldn't mind as much not being able to walk, but if I can never eat again, that will be unbearable."

My wonderful friend Sue Danaher is a speech therapist who I've known for years. We met because our children swam together on the same age-group team in Watertown. Sue inquired frequently about Alicia's progress with her swallowing function. She taught me many things about the particulars of this not-so-simple reflex, which most of us take for granted. Every time we take a single bite a complex sequence of actions begins and allows us to swallow.

Sue also passed along articles on the latest treatments being used to help people with dysphasia, or swallowing dysfunction. Being well read on all that was going on in her area of professional expertise, she told us about some of the research studies being done around the country and treatments that were on the cutting edge of her field. She encouraged me to look into this further.

Alicia's question of the day, all day, every day at that point was, "When do you think I will be able to eat again? Do you think I'll be able to?" Alicia's inability to eat became the priority, the situation that most needed to change.

Sue and I narrowed it down to researching the particulars of two different studies underway in the United States. One was in Chicago, the other in Cleveland. They shared similarities in the mechanism used to stimulate the nerves in the throat, epiglottis and esophagus. Both programs were showing dramatic results.

I also spoke with Alicia's speech therapist at Gaylord, and it didn't take long to see that we were all on the same page. We had exhausted every type of standard therapy in the area of dysphasia; we all agreed that making a move to one of the latest research programs producing some of the newer innovations in this area would be a good idea.

We chose the program at the Case Western University Hospital Health System in Cleveland. The study was seeking participants with severe dysphasia. Pediatric speech pathologist Marci Freed was having very good results with her method referred to as E-Stim.

The procedure involved placing electrodes near the ends of the five main cranial nerves that are involved in swallowing. A small current was then transmitted in sequence in order to stimulate the muscles involved in the swallowing process. The idea was to trigger the muscles to carry out their swallowing function.

I got in touch with Marci Freed's office at the beginning of December; they required some evaluations from anyone who had seen Alicia in regard to her swallowing function. Information was sent from Dr. Diane Fountas, her primary pediatrician, as well as speech pathologists at Yale and Gaylord. When all the information was reviewed, the group in Cleveland decided that Alicia would be a good candidate for their study. She'd had a devastating injury that left her with no swallowing function at all, yet she could communicate and cooperate with all aspects of this study. Many individuals with that extensive an injury also have problems thinking and communicating; Alicia was a helpful exception to the norm for them. She would be able to provide helpful feedback while participating in the research study.

Alicia was approved, and we were in line to start the study at 11 am on Dec. 26, 2002. Excitement built as we made arrangements for our trip out to Cleveland. The length of our stay there was not set in stone; it would depend on the progress Alicia was making. The usual length of stay was two to three weeks.

I lined up friends and family to help get Bryan and Crissy, to where they needed to go. The middle of basketball season meant they had busy sports schedules.

Accommodations while we were out there were a concern at first, but we soon learned that there was a Ronald McDonald House within a few blocks of Rainbow Babies and Children's Hospital, the part of UHHS where Marci Freed's office was. We made reservations with that RMD House, and then we were ready to go. Money raised by the Village Striders and at the Holy Cross Ziti Dinner that year not only paid for the van with the wheelchair lift that we bought, which was now going to get us where we needed to be, the funds also covered travel expenses and the cost of staying at the RMD House.

For the several weeks that we prepared to head for Cleveland, we were full of anticipation and quiet reservations about what we believed was a strong possibility for helping Alicia regain her swallowing function. All other priorities were tossed aside so that we could go and give Alicia the best chance to recover one of the "normal" things she missed the most—eating. Even Christmas that year lost a bit of its importance as we focused on preparation for our trip to Cleveland.

In a family not unfamiliar with adventure, this trip was exciting to both of us. Alicia always loved to go for long rides and found ways to occupy herself on any type of ride. I had traveled with the kids many times when they were young, visiting friends from out of state. That was always something that they looked forward to and enjoyed. This journey was no exception. We rigged up a television with a VHS tape player in it on top of a commode in the van and brought all of Alicia's favorite movies with us. The large conversion van with a wheelchair lift that we had purchased now became the perfect vehicle for a serious road trip.

We were entirely organized and ready to go days before Christmas. We planned to celebrate Christmas with a family meal and spending time together before we left for a fair amount of time. A few days prior to our planned trip the weather reports started to speak of the possibility of a winter storm coming from the Midwest and hitting the Northeast on Christmas Day.

We weren't all that worried; we figured we had a heavy vehicle with adequate snow tires. I felt very comfortable about driving to Cleveland, even if there was to be a bit of snow. I have always loved driving in the snow, as well as taking part in an adventure, so in my mind the trip was actually starting to sound a bit more exciting. Paul wasn't exactly thrilled with the idea of Alicia and I being on such a long road trip in the middle of a snow storm, but he knew better than to try and talk a stubborn Irish woman out of anything she had set her mind to.

On Christmas morning the forecasts started to show the storm was increasing in strength. Now a major snow event was expected to dump a few feet of snow from the Midwest up through New England. Initially the snow was supposed to start in the late afternoon, but as flakes began to fall in the late morning we started an all-out race to get out the door.

I called my wonderful friend Elaine, who lived up around the corner. We had been in frequent contact throughout Alicia's hospital stay and once she was home. Elaine, Tom and her kids were the amazing friends who practically adopted Bryan throughout Alicia's stay in the hospital. Elaine had invited both of the kids to come up after school and to hang out and eat over anytime. From what I understand, Bryan took them up on the offer as frequently as possible and would be found there most nights, having supper with their family and then hanging out, doing whatever they were doing for the evening.

As we'd prepared for the trip, Elaine, Sue and a few other friends had talked about joining us for the ride out to Cleveland. Being such an open-ended trip, however, made it impossible for anyone to get the time off to travel or stay with us there.

I called Elaine around noon and told her we were going to have to head out of town in a hurry in order to make it to Cleveland by noon the next day. At least we could make progress, even if it was going to take longer than expected. Her husband Tom came down and helped Paul quickly load up the van. We tucked Alicia in with her wheelchairs, medical equipment and enough clothes and supplies to last for several weeks. At that point Alicia's mobility was very limited; she still had a tracheostomy and was fed exclusively by g-tube. We had to bring enough of the tube feedings and trach equipment to last for potentially three weeks or so. Finally, after good-byes that seemed too short and some last-minute preps, we got on the road at just around 2 pm.

The thought of postponing the adventure that represented Alicia's best hope for being able to eat again never crossed our minds. We were entirely blind to what problems might lay ahead. I just knew we had to get there. Nothing would stop us.

As Alicia and I left our driveway the ground was already covered with a blanket of snow, which was coming down more heavily as the minutes passed. We knew we were going to have to take it easy. We took about an hour to get through Danbury, a trip that usually took about a half an hour. I knew now that we were looking at doubling our expected times, especially in areas where it was snowing.

Sleet came down with the snow, and we began to have problems with the windshield and the wipers freezing as we crossed the border into New York state. I could no longer see the lines in the road at all. We couldn't have gone any faster than 30 mph the entire way though the state, and visibility was becoming more of a problem with every mile.

Deep down inside, somewhere in my sane mind, I was getting a bit scared about being out there in those treacherous conditions. Alicia, on the other hand, was oblivious to the dangerous situation on the roads. As I looked through the rearview mirror, I saw her sitting and watching a video we had turned on as we left the house. I could imagine her excitement just under the surface, born of a new hope that we would find answers in Cleveland that would perhaps allow her to be able to eat again sometime soon. On we drove.

As we came upon the fifth exit in Pennsylvania, I saw a state police car up ahead, directing the few cars on the highway to get off at that exit. There was just over a foot of new snow on the ground, with another two feet expected before the morning. Conditions continued to deteriorate, forcing them to close the highway. We were directed to the only open establishment at the exit, a convenience store gas station. About fifty cars filled the parking lot, as well as others parked along the main road before and after the entrance to the driveway. It was impossible to get into the parking lot, so I parked strategically out along the main road with the van pointing toward the highway. I talked it over with Alicia and then made my way to the convenience store to try and get any info I could about what was happening. I left the van running so that Alicia could stay warm, with a window open a crack for ventilation.

In the store the floors were covered with people laying down on blankets and coats. The word was that the highway was going to be closed throughout the night. I made my way back to the van to let Alicia know what was going on. We had no choice other than to wait it out...or did we?

After examining the map at length, I found an alternate route that would take us on some secondary roads to route 80, which ran parallel to 84 about sixty miles south of where we were. We had heard that route 80 was still open. I was very conscious of having to be in Cleveland at 11 am for our initial interview/exam in order to start the program on time. The twenty-sixth was a Friday; if we didn't get going this week it was unclear when we could begin, as initial exams were only offered twice a week.

I was very anxious about the situation and felt that we absolutely needed to be there by the next day at 11 am. We were only about a quarter of the way through our trip.

I made a few phone calls to touch base with my friends back home. A team of cheerleaders back in Connecticut waited at the other end of the phone to hear about what was going on, as well to provide any help they could. I discussed the idea of making my way along the back roads in order to drive down to route 80. The plan we decided on was to wait until midnight and see if there were any updates about the highway possibly reopening.

Just before midnight I made my way back to the store and asked about the situation. Nothing had changed; the snow continued to fall heavily. We decided to try plan B. The roads were slick but passable, and I took it slow. I followed the map, and I was making decent progress south on route 196. At about the thirty-mile mark after our departure from the store, we started to notice that we were making a fairly steady assent, at first gradually, then increasingly steep. Visibility was poor as we made our way down the back roads in the middle of the night. It looked as though they had been plowed, but new snow was piling up. We tried to make it from route 196 to 940W, which would have taken us out onto 380 for a quick jaunt to route 80. We found that 940 was impassible, so we headed back to the middle of a town that was supposed to have a right turn that would take us on 611S. We went through the town without seeing the turn off; everything was covered with snow, including signs. I decided to turn around and make our way back about a mile to the town.

As we approached from the opposite direction the sign was clearly visible. I attempted to make a left turn onto route 611, but noticed as I approached the corner that the road had perhaps not been plowed at all. The van was a fairly heavy vehicle; I felt that once we got around the corner and started steadily up the road we would be fine. Several attempts to get around the corner proved fruitless; there were huge piles of snow on either side of the road. I was about to accept the apparent impossibility to make the turn under those conditions, but decided to give it one more try. Backing as far as possible to get the best angle ahead of me, I made a run at the hill through a very narrow opening to the unplowed road. The van immediately started to skid off the road to the right, and I found myself jammed sideways in an approximately four-foot high snow pile at the side of a dark road in the middle of the eastern Pennsylvania mountains.

If I'd had one shred of sense in my otherwise focused mind, I would have recognized it as a dangerous and perhaps losing battle. Instead, I saw only a challenge. I got out of the van and made my way through knee-high snow to the back of the van to get the shovel packed inside. When I say packed, I am talking crammed in, along with all manner of supplies—full-to-the-brim-with-stuff packed. I opened the door... Yes, there is a God; the shovel was right inside. Thank you, Paul, for the nice packing job!

Partway through the shoveling-out-the-van event, my friend Sue called to see what kind of progress we were making. Hmm... Tough question, considering it was about 1 am and I had fallen off the grid somewhere in a state that up until then only seemed annoying because it meant a forever-long drive to pass through. Well, new day, new perspective, I suppose. I talked to Sue as I shoveled my way out of the pile of snow that was snuggly wrapped around "the gladiator." On to plan C.

After digging for a good half an hour, and a couple of tries of maneuvering the van forwards and backwards, eventually we were freed. I made my way back along the same roads that we'd come down and then took a bit of a longer road that carried us to the next exit on the highway. It was 3 am, and they had just opened the highway. Perfect! No time lost—just a little sanity.

There were a few more delays as we made our way down route 81 from Scranton to route 80. Just after Wilkes-Barre, the warning signs on the highway started to flash, indicating that the highway was closed. Please get off the next exit. *Are you kidding me?* Figuring I had only a few miles to go to the merge with 80, I kept moving. (I only mention this because I am sure we are safely past the statute of limitations period for such an offense.)

The conditions on 80 were much better, allowing us to maintain a steady pace. We arrived at the Pennsylvania/ Ohio border at around 9 am. The roads were still bad, but my only concern was making it to Cleveland in under two hours, a feat that seemed nearly impossible. I kept moving and tried to contact Marci Freed's office to ask if we should come, as we were running a bit behind schedule. Her office contacted her and they got back to me at about 9:30, saying that I would be fine if I could make it in by noon. That phone call was the last time my speedometer read anything close to the speed limit, by the way.

We approached Cleveland from the northeast side of the city and made it inside the city limits by 11:50. At each stop light, I reexamined the map of the city. As we made our way down the main route toward the hospital, coming up fast on the noon hour, I realized we were not going to make it. I called the office and was given the news that we would not be able to be seen that day. They would call me on Monday to set up a time for our screening next week.

Now, to most people that might not seem like too big of a deal. After all, within a couple of days we would hear about when we could start the process. However, we did not come under the category of "most people." I had been driving in a blizzard for just under twenty-four hours, awake for more than thirty. I had driven about 650 miles with my precious cargo Alicia who, most importantly, hadn't eaten a thing in the fashion that she preferred in more than ten months. I was totally frazzled, frustrated and in tears.

To make a long story short, I would have contacted the president of the United States if it would have helped at that point. Instead I contacted our pediatrician, Dr. Diane Fountas, who in turn contacted Marci Freed's office, telling them of our overwhelming frustration and intense journey. Within an hour we were called and told that we had an appointment for Saturday morning at nine o'clock. Thank you, Diane!

Little did we know when we checked into the Ronald McDonald House that we would be staying there for more than a month. We went back and forth to the hospital every day as Alicia underwent the E-Stim treatments.

We can't say enough about the wonderful treatment that Alicia received while in Cleveland or the amazing hospitality that was provided by the volunteers who ran the Ronald McDonald House. The setup there was amazing; with all the amenities and comforts it would provide, we may as well have been staying at a five-star hotel.

We explored the area in our spare time and had many opportunities to relax and enjoy each other's company. Although it snowed twenty-eight of the thirty-one days we were in Cleveland, our stay gifted us with hope; we were grateful to be a part of the whole program there.

Although Alicia underwent treatments every day, no change in her swallowing function became apparent, other than a few hopeful moments along the way. We drove home from Cleveland on Jan 28 with little hope there would be any change. We flew back a week later for a full evaluation, including imaging and barium swallows, a test that uses a special dye to track the movement of liquid during swallowing. The X-ray machine produces a series of pictures of the barium liquid as it passes through the mouth and progresses to the stomach. As Alicia attempted to swallow the liquid, the images clearly showed that no progress had been made. Alicia continued to have absolutely no swallowing function whatsoever.

Alicia in the foyer of Rainbow Babies and Children's Hospital, Cleveland - January 2003

After coming home from Cleveland, Alicia continued speech therapy, as well as PT and OT, at Gaylord Rehabilitation Hospital. We appreciated getting life back on track, even though we were not entirely sure what this new track entailed.

She then made a choice to continue with her life's dream of completing high school and going to college to become a teacher, rather than concentrate on continued therapy. Her plans were taking shape to continue at Holy Cross in the fall so that she could eventually graduate from high school.

CHAPTER 17

Back to School

IT ALWAYS SEEMS IMPOSSIBLE,
UNTIL IT'S DONE.
~Nelson Mandela~

ALICIA HAD ALWAYS DREAMED OF being a teacher.
I believe she was in second grade when she started telling
us of the career path she wanted to take. As she was
making her way through her junior year in high school,
she had started to think about colleges that she might be
interested in for pursuing her chosen area of study as an
early childhood education teacher. Although life had
taken a dramatic detour for Alicia, she was adamant about
continuing on with her goal, if it were at all possible.

Clearly there were many things to consider as she
aimed at returning to school. She was in a wheelchair, had
limited fine-motor skills, as well as a difficult time
carrying out the activities of daily living. Her voice was
very quiet, making it difficult for her to communicate.
We weren't sure if there had been any other cognitive
changes; a full neuro-psych evaluation was conducted,
which she passed with flying colors.

We met with the special education team from
Watertown, who advised us on the best plan for Alicia to

achieve her short- and long-term goals. We met with guidance counselors and administrators to assess how Alicia might be able to continue at Holy Cross. One of the math teachers, Mrs. Shove, offered to meet with Alicia after school a few days a week in order to help her complete her junior year math requirements. Alicia also was tutored as an outpatient at Gaylord in English once a week, and started to complete her junior year history requirement at home with a private tutor.

In the fall of 2002, while catching up with her academic coursework, she also decided to carry on as co-captain of her swim team at Holy Cross. She had a great love for swimming, as well as for her coach, Todd Dyer, and her fellow swim teammates. She remained close friends with several of the girls on the team and tried to get to some practices, as well as all of the team's home meets and most of their away meets. Alicia has a wonderful sense of loyalty and devotion to her friends and wanted to remain a support to them during the season following the one that she had been so involved in as a junior, when they won the league championship.

One day we were informed that a reporter from the local newspaper would be at practice to take a picture and talk with Alicia. He came and sat down with Alicia and Mr. Dyer, and an article appeared in the *Republican-American* a week or so later.

This is a portion of the article, written by Joe Palladino, staff writer at the paper.

Inspiration for Cross Swimmers

With her arm wrapped around her mom's shoulder, Holy Cross senior Alicia Townsend begins a task that you and I take for granted. Slowly, methodically, Townsend places one foot in front of the other. Carefully, cautiously, she walks down six stairs to get to the pool deck at Kennedy High School. She once bounded this stairwell. Now it is another test in a life that has become one enormous hurdle.

The 17-year-old Watertown resident, and all NVL swimmer, and inductee into the National Honor Society, is a captain for the Crusaders swim team that will try and win its third straight Naugatuck Valley League championship later this week. But now Townsend is something she never wanted to be: a fighter, a role model, an inspiration, and maybe even, as her mom calls her, a miracle girl...

..."Her goal," noted moist-eyed Cross swim captain Rachele Testa, "is to walk across that stage at Holy Cross on graduation night."

That miracle may be a ways off, but Townsend has managed to attend every Holy Cross home meet and most of the away meets. She'll be at her graduation, and on her feet too. Just one week ago, she realized a short-term dream when Dyer lifted her out of the wheelchair and carried her into the pool during practice.

"That was something she wanted to do," Testa added, "get back in the water. Seeing her in the pool brought tears to everyone's eyes."

Townsend isn't looking for tears. "I want to be the same kid I was before," she said. "For the team." That's why she parades with the team before each meet, riding in her chair while Cross sings its pep songs. She sits poolside, and joins in the handshake line. Teammates are in awe of her courage.

"She means everything to this team," said captain Meaghan Riley.

Alicia just wants to swim. "Well I don't know if I am an inspiration," she says of her teammates. "I just try to support them. I want to encourage them to try no matter what. I guess by my being there they kind of get the message."

Kind of.

And then she adds, "You don't know how much you love something until you cannot do it anymore."

We all say that, but they are just words. We don't have a clue about what they truly mean. Alicia Townsend knows. And when she says it, sitting in her chair, a tube sticking out of her throat, her mom helping her with the simplest of tasks, those words overwhelm. We can toss around other words like courage and inspiration, but we will never really know what those words mean.

Alicia Townsend knows.

Portions of the article reprinted with the permission of *Republican-American* in Waterbury, Connecticut.

The days seemed to fly by as we all adjusted to life with Alicia back home with us. She went to therapies at Gaylord during the week On the weekends she would either relax around the house or get out for a ride or a visit, catching up with old friends or just enjoying life as it came.

Alicia was asked to go to the senior prom by her good friend Alexei in the spring of 2003. They had known each other for about four years, having met on the Watertown Age Group swim team. Her friends Megan, Meaghan and Sarah all met at Meaghan's house prior to the prom for pictures. They had a great time together at the prom, and followed that up with an after-prom party at a local campground where they watched the sun come up.

Alicia and Alexei on the way to the Senior Prom Spring 2003.
(Alicia always insists on standing for pictures, although
still confined to a wheelchair.)

Alicia attended her friends' graduation, knowing that she would miss them as they moved on ahead of her in life by leaving for college, many of which were out of state. She attended one graduation party after another, enjoying time with her friends while they were still close by.

In the fall of 2003, Alicia went back to Holy Cross to finish her senior year. After assessing Alicia's academic status, we learned that she would only have to complete three courses to finish her senior year requirements. Never choosing the easy way out, Alicia decided to take several other classes that would expand her knowledge base; she was aiming at college after graduation. She also didn't think it was fair to not take the classes that everyone else was taking, so she decided to return to school in the fall to complete her senior year. Bryan was a sophomore that year and Crissy a freshman.

Alicia was sad not to have graduated with all of her friends but accepted that reality. She decided to keep moving with what she was capable of doing. Alicia attended school for half a day each day and handled all the new changes quite well. The school was very accommodating, moving classes that she had to attend to the first floor so that she could easily get to them. I believe Alicia was one of the few students with such a variety of medical needs, but everyone was extremely helpful about providing anything she needed to make things work as easily as possible. She had a motorized chair at that point and was able to get around the building without any trouble at all.

After school we would drive to Wallingford two to three days a week for her outpatient therapies. She tried whenever possible to attend sporting events that she enjoyed, especially swimming. She was inducted into the National Honor Society that year, for the second time. The first induction had been while she was in the hospital, unable to attend. She continued to make friends with her new classmates, although most of her good friends had graduated the previous year.

Alicia also went to the senior prom during her senior year. She had been good friends with Ken for years, and even though he had graduated the previous year he offered to accompany Alicia to her prom. She happily accepted, and many of her friends who still lived in the area came to the house on the afternoon of the prom to help her prepare. She had a great time, and she had no trouble finding partners to dance with all night.

Alicia and Ken ~ Senior Prom #2 (the dress is size 00, btw)

While we were overjoyed to realize all that Alicia had accomplished since her surgery, we were also looking ahead. Alicia continued to dream and to move forward with purpose, setting goals and pursuing them.

While enjoying each day, we talked often about what would come next. One of her goals was to get as close as she could to her previous levels of functioning, but we also had to be realistic; Alicia had to work very hard to make any progress.

Alicia always had been diligent in the area of academics; that certainly had not changed. She studied hard and went above and beyond as she completed her senior courses. As she came to the end of her high school years, she looked forward to moving on, as most of her friends already had. She looked forward to starting college.

As graduation approached, excitement was in the air. Alicia attended all the practices, and teachers and administrators tried to figure out how to include Alicia in the graduation ceremony. Alicia had hoped to be walking at that point. Although she had worked extremely hard at physical therapy and increased her strength, her cerebellar injury meant she continued to have no equilibrium. She would not be able to walk onto the stage to receive her diploma. Two of Alicia's favorite teachers, Mrs. Ann Estrada and Mr. Dennis Killian, had a meeting with administrators to discuss a way for Alicia to receive her diploma.

The auditorium filled on June 6, 2004, graduation day at Holy Cross. Paul and I, as well as my mother, Theresa and Megan Moynihan, sat about halfway down in seats to the right of the stage. The graduates filed in as the school band played "Pomp and Circumstance." We looked on as Alicia was pushed to her spot at the end of the center aisle. The graduates were in line alphabetically and a space was made for Alicia's wheelchair so she could be easily wheeled down the aisle to approach the stage.

After listening to speeches by the principal, the valedictorian and salutatorian, the delivery of diplomas commenced. One by one names were called out and students walked up the steps onto the stage to receive their diplomas. My family and I were in tears when we spotted Alicia being pushed down the aisle toward the stage. We saw her round the corner just in front of the stage and be wheeled to within two feet of the steps. Mrs. Estrada and Mr. Killian helped her lock the brakes and then assisted Alicia to a standing position. As Sr. Denise announced, "Alicia Rose Townsend," with Mrs. Estrada on her right and Mr. Killian on her left, they walked her up the four steps and across the stage to where she was able to reach out her hand and accept her diploma. The entire auditorium of people rose to their feet and thunderously applauded as Alicia slowly walked back across the stage and down the steps to her wheelchair, escorted by two of her favorite teachers. She had done it; she was now back on track for achieving her dreams.

June 6, 2004 – Graduation Day

Alicia with Sarah, Megan and Mr. Killian

Theresa, Margie, Paul, my Mom and myself

Alicia and Mrs. Ann Estrada

CHAPTER 18

Chasing the Dream

"THE SKY IS NOT MY LIMIT, I AM…"
~T.F. Hodge~

DURING ALICIA'S SENIOR YEAR IN HIGH school we had researched colleges that provided disability services. One day I came across the heading Disability-Friendly Colleges on the computer, with a list of the top one hundred disabled-friendly colleges in the country, including ratings and explanations. They were rated not only on how much of the campus was accessible but also on what types of services were available for individuals with all types of disabilities. We had never heard of such a concept and were so happy to see that there was so much out there for students with all varieties of physical, mental or learning limitations.

We traveled to a number of schools on the list that were reasonable day trips away. We checked out the campuses of Hofstra, Plymouth State, Southern Connecticut State University, Keene State and Mitchell College. There were pros and cons to each, so we decided to continue the search.

As we were planning our first long-distance trip to the University of Illinois at Urbana Champaign, voted the number-one Disabled Friendly College that year, we learned about another school that we would be passing by on our way.

Several families in the Village Striders had been inquiring frequently about how things had been going with Alicia. Our close friend Berta Andrulis had heard about our search for schools that might be better able to accommodate Alicia's needs. She suggested that we take a look at Wright State University in Fairborn, Ohio, just outside of Dayton. Her brother Greg had been a soccer coach there for years before he left to take the position of head coach of the Columbus Crew in Columbus, Ohio. He had told Berta that Wright State offered very advanced programs to meet the needs of disabled students and the campus was 100-percent accessible.

So in the spring of 2006 we headed out on a road trip to the University of Illinois, as well as Wright State. We were impressed by the services offered by UOI to even the most severely handicapped students. We were told that they had a dorm that housed students with a variety of physical disabilities and medical needs. Personal assistants and medical personnel were on staff for these students. Their facilities were able to accommodate students who were in wheelchairs, had spinal cord injuries, brain injuries, were g-tube fed, or had oxygen needs, even students on ventilators.

As we made our way into the Midwest along route 70, we decided to take a quick look at Wright State University. We would practically pass right by it on the highway near Dayton. We made a quick drive-by review of that campus first and planned to check it out in depth on our way back from Urbana Champaign. From the minute we saw the Wright State campus we were impressed, even though we did not, as I recall, even get out of the van. It was an open, modern, attractive campus and made a very strong first impression. We made our way back onto route 70 and drove another five to six hours to Illinois.

After driving through hundreds of miles of open fields with 360 degrees of visible horizon, we were happy to finally see civilization as we approached the Indiana-Illinois state line. Almost as if it had popped up out of the fields, we could see up ahead of us something that appeared to be a city. We found out as we approached that it was in fact the University of Illinois at Urbana Champaign. The huge campus indeed had all the hustle and bustle of a large city, reminding us both of Boston as we drove into and around street upon street of brownstone brick buildings and narrow one-way roads.

It was early evening as we arrived on campus. We decided to make a tour of the area, stay the night and then meet with the director of Disability Services the next day.

We located the dorm building we had been told about and then drove around to get a feel for the area. We decided to get something to eat and then find a hotel. As we were eating, Alicia informed me that she felt bad. She thought that it would be a waste of time to stick around to talk to the Disability Services coordinator the next day; she had "absolutely no intention of going to this school."

Hmmm, okay!

Actually, I was quite impressed with what I had seen of the campus, but Alicia insisted that the campus was much too big for her liking. She probably wouldn't feel comfortable there, especially since it was so far away from home. Seriously?!?!

There was still a little bit of daylight left, so we decided to head east out of town and get as close as we could to Ohio; we would take a look at Wright State the next day.

As we once again approached the Wright State campus, we both felt comfortable and had a good feeling about the possibilities there. There were many major pros to the school. The campus was beautiful to look at, with an underground tunnel system that connected most of the academic buildings on campus, as well as the Student Union and one of the dorms. It also had a very accommodating Disability Services Department. Our friend Berta's brother Greg lived in the area, and that added an extra degree of comfort to Alicia being so far from home.

We met with one of the staff of the Disabilities Department, who informed us that Wright State had the largest percentage of physically handicapped students in the country, comprising 9 percent of the student population. They also offered a variety of varsity sports adapted for that very active population of the student body. There were support groups, recreation and clubs for students with disabilities. A dorm close to the student union housed many wheelchair-bound residents on the first floor. Needs stations were located around campus and in the student union to assist with personal needs, as well as any problems that a student might encounter during the day. Someone always was available to repair wheelchairs and other medical equipment. Personal assistants were available through the school and provided hundreds of hours of care each day to students around campus who were in need of assistance. The entire campus was

100-percent accessible: a ramp was next to every staircase, all doors had automatic pad access and all bathrooms offered many handicapped-accessible stalls. The staff we met with were amazingly helpful and personable.

Alicia and I were thrilled to have found this school. We will be indebted forever to the Andrulises for telling us about and encouraging us to take a look at Wright State University. We made our way back home, thrilled to have found such a college. Considering all of Alicia's needs, we believed WSU would be just the right fit.

Most of the summer involved preparing for the beginning of the next phase of her life. We met again with Diane Pollutro from the Connecticut Bureau of Rehabilitation Services (BRS). This state agency was responsible for coordinating Alicia's plan to continue her education after high school. We had presented all aspects of our search to find a school that would be able to meet all of Alicia's needs, while providing her with the education necessary to earn a degree in the field of her choice. While schools in Connecticut did offer an Early Childhood Education degree, none of them offered the same level of services for the disabled that Wright State University did. Mrs. Pollutro was a major advocate for us as we sought approval from the state of Connecticut to help us pay for educational expenses at a school in Ohio. Luckily, we had seen how advanced Wright State was in providing services, personal assistants and other programs geared exclusively for disabled students. As it turned out, BRS was able to pay for the majority of school costs, as they would have had she attended school in Connecticut.

In mid-August we made our way out to Wright State for the orientation for the new students who would be receiving services from the Department of Disability Services. If we had not already been amazingly impressed by all the school had to offer, we definitely would have been in awe after the orientation program. During the two-day orientation, we toured the campus, spoke with financial aid officers, spoke with staff from the Office of Disability Services and visited the dorm where Alicia would be living. The thought of Alicia going to school there was becoming exciting to both of us.

If I sound as though it was easy to think of Alicia being seven hundred miles away, let me assure you that it was not. I knew, though, that pursuing her dream was very important for her to be able to enjoy life. I also realized that if there was any chance for Alicia to truly thrive, it would be as an independent woman doing what she had always wanted to do. Once again I had to learn to let go.

School would start the day after Labor Day, so we gave ourselves a few days to get out there and move everything in. With cautious anticipation and a tad of excitement, we started to pack. Although we had heard that a student usually over-packs for their actual needs, we filled the van to the brim with every possible thing that Alicia would ever think of needing. You couldn't fit another piece of paper in the back of the van; we barely fit Alicia in.

Alicia had half of a dorm room; her space to hold all of her stuff in, including her bed, desk and amply large wardrobe, was approximately ten by twelve feet. We brought all manner of medical supplies, along with the usual things: clothes, entertainment necessities and school supplies. Her room was full to the brim—under the bed, on top of the wardrobe, shelves on every flat surface. We made more than a few trips to Meier's, the Midwest's answer to a Super Walmart, as we set up her room.

For three days we unpacked the van, arranging and rearranging. We bought more stacked drawers, filled them up, and rearranged some more. In the end, hers was the ultimate in efficiently arranged and stocked dorm rooms. We had a lot of fun too. When it came time for me to drive home without my girl, sadness set in for both of us. We had been together virtually every day for the last two and a half years. A lot of that time was spent in hospitals under stressful circumstances and in dealing with the difficult task of getting on with a very changed life situation. We had become very close; we both knew we would miss our time together. I did feel good about the fact that she would have personal assistants helping her for several hours a day or more if she needed, starting the next day. There was amazingly helpful staff in the dorm that was eager to help in any way.

Alicia had been so excited about the idea of moving along with her life and doing the things that she wanted. We sort of ignored the fact that it was going to be a huge adjustment for both of us.

We made plans for the first trip that I would make out to visit her, in a month; we could talk any time before then. A new, custom motorized wheelchair was being made that would be ready in just about three weeks. At the time she was using a jazzy chair that we had bought from a friend of Paul's, and Alicia had learned to maneuver it quite well in the past year and a half. We spoke of the arrangements for the visit often in the hours before I got into the van and started to drive away.

Saying good-bye to Alicia as she sat in her wheelchair out in front of her dorm with tears streaming down her face was one of the hardest things I ever had to do. As I drove away I thought to myself, *What kind of mother leaves a child who can do almost nothing for herself more or less alone, in a totally new place over seven hundred miles from home?* I cried all the way to mid-Pennsylvania.

To say that Alicia had a tough adjustment to make to college life, mostly because of the distance from home, was an understatement. She called frequently, crying and saying she wanted to come home. Although deep down inside I wanted the same thing, I always reminded her of her excitement about getting on with life and going to college. She usually would agree and end our conversations on a more positive note.

Her new wheelchair arrived and I drove out to bring it to Alicia and stay for a long weekend. It was wonderful to see her and learn that she had been making friends and was doing well in all her classes. She showed me where all her classes were around campus and introduced me to her friends. We went to the store and bought new supplies and had a very nice weekend. Many times during the weekend Alicia spoke of how difficult being so far away from home was.

As the first quarter went along, being far from home only became more difficult for Alicia. She decided to come back to Connecticut and go to Southern Connecticut State University in New Haven for the spring semester. She returned to Connecticut in early December, so she had plenty of time to make arrangements to get admitted to Southern in January. We went to the campus and spoke with the staff of the Disabilities Department and admissions. Soon Alicia moved into the dorm and was on her way down another path, her long-term goals still in view.

Being close to home was much easier for Alicia, although we all noticed that she had become noticeably more independent. She was able to advocate for herself as well as initiate all plans and preparations that needed to be made. She had grown to be quite self-reliant during those three months at Wright State, learning the ropes of dealing with life in a wheelchair from other students who were in the same position.

The first semester at Southern went by quickly. Alicia came home most weekends. She also restarted therapies at Gaylord at their New Haven facility. She arranged for rides by chair car from the school campus to Gaylord's satellite office once a week. Things were going smoothly, just on a different track.

Prior to Alicia's surgery she had been swimming on a very competitive swim team at the pool at Southern. She and her friend Meaghan had driven down there for each practice night in November and December 2001. Alicia had, as always, befriended the coaches she swam for. Now that she was on campus in 2005, she made her way back to the pool to visit with the two coaches she knew from the swim team. Her tracheostomy had been removed and repaired in the fall of 2003. The opening in her throat was now sealed and some reconstructive surgery was done that closed the opening on the inside and out. Alicia now wanted to get back into the water. Although she was unable to walk, she had gained a lot of strength and thought that swimming again wasn't out of the question.

We got together with the head coach Tim Quill to make her case. He agreed to let Alicia come to the pool to practice with the team. We had a custom life jacket made for Alicia, which allowed her freedom of movement but kept her safely afloat.

She practiced with the team that semester, and Tim asked Alicia if she wanted to be a member of Southern Connecticut State University's swim team in the fall of 2006. Alicia, of course, agreed and became a member of the team. The school purchased a lift to assist Alicia with getting in and out of the pool.

She was quite frustrated that she couldn't swim as she had prior to the surgery, but she continued to practice with the team each day and attended most of their swim meets. She missed several meets because there had been snow the previous night and the maintenance department had not yet shoveled the ramp leading out of her dorm building.

She felt frustrated that she wasn't able to help the team with her swimming abilities. However, in 2005 she did help the Southern Connecticut State University Swim Team become ranked as an Academic All-American team with her grade point average of 4.0. That's my girl!

CHAPTER 19

The Most Wonderful Time of the Year!

AND NOW WE STEP
TO THE RHYTHM OF MIRACLES.
~Aberjhani~

NOT TOO LONG AFTER RETURNING from Cleveland in the spring of 2003, we had set our sights on another possibility for addressing Alicia's swallowing problem. We were not about to give up on her dream to eat again.

In the fall of 2003 my friend Sue found us another study. The National Institute of Health (NIH) in Bethesda, Maryland was seeking candidates with severe dysphasia for a study. They were working on the development of an internal device that would aid in the swallowing process. The study was being performed at the main campus of the NIH, just outside of Washington, DC. I made several phone calls to inquire about the study and to tell them a little about Alicia and her situation.

Once again a vast amount of information needed to be collected, this time to be sent to NIH in order to initiate the process. The most recent history and physical done by her primary-care pediatrician and physiatrist, as well as a recent evaluation by a speech pathologist, needed to be completed and sent. We established a connection with the speech pathology department at Yale to have the evaluation performed. All the information was gathered and sent to Lisa, our liaison for the study being conducted by the Otolaryngology Department at NIH.

The months came and went. Alicia's time was filled with all kinds of activity as she continued with school. She was testing her limits and exploring her interests in her new world, getting used to life away from home. It was a huge adjustment.

Since she was living back in Connecticut, we decided to wait for a semester break to make our way to NIH for the clinical part of the study. We flew down for two days for the initial evaluation on November 21, 2005. A shuttle picked us up as we arrived at the Baltimore/Washington Airport and took us directly to Building 10 on the sprawling NIH campus in Bethesda. We met Lisa, who explained our schedule for the next two days.

Alicia was admitted into the hospital there while the evaluation was done. A thorough battery of tests and imaging protocols were performed to evaluate her general state of health and her limitations, as well as her degree of function, or rather non-function, in regard to swallowing. The results of the preliminary testing showed that Alicia had no swallowing function whatsoever and was unable to protect her airway while eating.

The scope and plan for involvement in the study were explained. She would return when her schedule allowed and take part in a two day trial that would evaluate whether she would be a candidate for the use of a device they were in the process of researching. This device would some day assist individuals with severe swallowing dysfunction to be able to eat again. Alicia and I agreed that there were virtually no risks compared to the possible benefits that could be expected, so we decided that it would be a good idea for Alicia to participate. All the papers were signed, and we were given a tentative date to return for the actual trial.

My friend Sue joined Alicia and I as we returned to NIH on Dec.20, 2005, an exciting trip for us all. We once again gathered every ounce of hope and took it with us to Maryland. Our hope for Alicia eating again bolstered our spirits as we started our road trip together to Bethesda.

Sue and Alicia in the waiting room at the National Institute of Health, December 2005

The two-day trial for the Vital Stim study would determine candidacy for permanent electrode implants. Alicia was the only participant there on those days.

She received the attention of all the major players gathered to carry out the meticulously engineered criteria of the procedure. The study team was comprised of an Otolaryngologist, speech pathologists and a biomedical engineer.

We arrived quite early that morning and once again made our way to the otolaryngology floor in Building 10. Lisa came out to greet us in the assigned area and led us to a room down the hall. As we entered the room for the research study, we were awed by the setup. There was one chair in the center and the wall to the right held a floor-to-ceiling conglomeration of the most high-tech components any of us had ever seen.

Alicia was in good spirits and joked around with members of the study team. As we arrived, the equipment was set up, calibrated, and tested. Alicia was helped into the central chair. Sue and I were allowed to remain and were given comfortable stools set off to the side from where we could observe.

A nice thing about teaching institutions is that the researchers love to talk about and explain what they are doing. Sue and I are both in the medical field; we soaked up the information and enjoyed every minute of it.

On the first day, the ENT doctor used the electromyogram (EMG), which detects muscle activity to locate the muscle pairs that contribute to swallowing. Then he numbed the area with lidocaine. Five pairs of muscle groups innervated by five different cranial nerves were located, and electrodes were inserted. Through an amplifier, the electrodes emitted small electrical impulses that stimulated the nerve endings. A particular muscular reaction confirmed the placement of each electrode, and then the next set was inserted. Wires protruding from Alicia's neck connected to wires that were attached to a button that Alicia held, as well as to a series of wires connected to the computer. The researchers measured and recorded everything that happened.

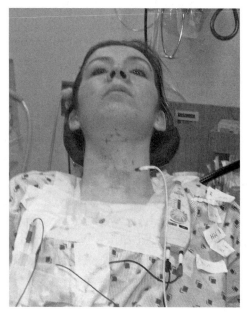

Please work, please work!

The purpose of the calibrations was to see if Alicia was able to initiate a swallow and then press the button within a certain amount of time. When initiated, the probes would measure the strength of the impulse given and her resulting ability to swallow.

The time it took for Alicia to press the button after she initiated a swallow was important. After her brain stem and cerebellar injury, there was a delay in the process of anything Alicia wanted to do. She might not have been considered as a candidate for such a device if she were unable to press a button to initiate a sequence of electrical impulses in the right amount of time.

This sequence was initiated by a pacemaker, for lack of a better word, created by the team of scientists to assist individuals like Alicia without any swallowing function. The device's implanted electrodes would trigger the muscles in her throat to carry out the proper sequence in order to eat.

As the actual practice attempts began, Dr. Ludlow would verbally cue Alicia about what to do. She was given several practice runs at initiating a swallow and then pressing the button, followed by a resting period in between. She was given twenty-five practice times to do the entire scenario. With each attempt, all manner of data was being collected, correlated, displayed, and recorded.

As Sue and I looked on, we had the impression that no matter how hard and quickly she tried, there was a significant time lapse between Alicia's initiation of the swallow and hitting the switch. We felt twinges of anxiety for her, which the two of us acknowledged through glances.

On the second day, the same preparations were carried out; the entire process was repeated and officially recorded as data for the trial. In the second part of the study that day, though, the actual swallow function was viewed under fluoroscopy and was taped. Sue and I looked on in silence, peeking as best we could at the screens that displayed what Alicia was actually doing as she attempted to swallow the radiopaque materials that included liquids of various thicknesses.

Swallows were successful with three pairs of muscles only, and two complete swallows were noted. The team was impressed with the improvements from the practice attempts the day before and verbalized optimism with what they saw. Alicia was told that all the data would be reviewed. The candidates for the permanent implants would be chosen in April, after a blind review by each team member.

After we wrapped up the testing that afternoon and said our farewells to the doctors and staff, we went for a bit of a tour of the place. We enjoyed each other's company, but silently we each tried to draw conclusions for ourselves on how everything had gone. Alicia broke into the silence at one point and commented that she was not sure that she would be satisfied with a permanent implant as a way to help her swallow.

We had a nice ride back to Connecticut together, as always enjoying the support and caring that we all shared. How grateful we were to Sue for not only letting us know about this study but also for joining us on our trip down to the trial.

We arrived home late on Dec 22. The next day in the afternoon, Alicia asked, as she often did, if she could try to swallow a little ice cream. "Of course," was my usual response. Ice cream would more or less slide right down the back of her throat, and by then Alicia was good at protecting her airway. Her strong cough would easily clear anything that happened to slip down the wrong way.

I was downstairs when I heard her yell, "Hey, Ma, can I try some more? I think it went down real easy." When I brought her another scoop of ice cream she informed me that she thought she had actually swallowed it "on purpose." Hmm...

After three years, eight months, and eight days, Alicia ate. She ate ice cream, followed by a slice of the pizza for supper. The next evening was Christmas Eve, and Alicia ate a bit of everything on the table at my sister Theresa's house, where we went for our holiday get-together.

We called it "The Christmas Miracle."

CHAPTER 20

Wright Back to School…

GO CONFIDENTLY IN THE DIRECTION
OF YOUR DREAMS.
LIVE THE LIFE YOU HAVE IMAGINED.
~Henry David Thoreau~

ALICIA RETURNED TO SCHOOL AT SCSU for the spring semester of 2006 a happy woman. Able to eat and drink again, she no longer had to be fed by g-tube. She used the meal plan at school for the first time and was thrilled. She also able to participate in social activities that she previously had been unable to.

I received a phone call one night from her resident advisor (RA), asking me to come and pick Alicia up from school. Her new-found ability to drink had gotten her into unfamiliar territory. Alicia, who had been quieter and more on the shy side since her surgery, was quite verbal when I arrived at 1 am to pick her up from Southern. She could not understand what the problem was and insisted that she was fine. It was probably not such a good idea to have a couple and then drive your motorized wheelchair around inside the dorm building. I convinced her to come home and sleep it off rather than continuing the discussion, and we all considered it a lesson learned.

Alicia became more familiar with her new life and how to deal with her limitations, as well as how to use her new-found strengths. She was not the same girl who went off to college two years before. She was now independent, excelling academically and always making new friends. She also had become a bit of an activist, advocating for herself as well as others in the disabled community.

In the spring of 2006 Alicia decided that she wanted to return to Wright State University in the fall. She started forming dreams and ideas as soon as the decision had been made. She wrapped up her year at Southern in May, enjoyed the summer with family and friends who were also home from college and prepared to go back to Ohio in August. She arranged to live in a new dorm, one that would be a bit more of a challenge because it was farther out from the center of campus, but it seemed more appealing to her. Alicia was excited about returning to the school that she had enjoyed in many ways, better prepared than in 2005 to be so far from home.

Alicia planned on joining the adapted swim team there, which she did shortly after arriving that fall. She also joined a few clubs so that she could get involved in reaching out to the community. The Circle K Club, college's version of the Key Club, was very active in a variety of volunteer services that reached out to the surrounding community.

On the last week of August we made our way back to Wright State University, the van packed a little more realistically than the first time. Moving in was, for me anyway, a lot more fun than the first time. Less stuff equaled more fun, as any parent who has moved their child into a college dorm will agree. There were no tears as I drove away from Alicia that time. None that we saw, that is.

Alicia called often to let me know how things were going and keep me updated on all that she was involved in. She joined the adapted swim team immediately; practices were held three times a week. She was able to do her favorite stroke, freestyle, but she also was putting a lot of effort into improving her back and breast strokes, as well as flip turns. She remained on the team for several months, but often expressed her frustration over not being able to do the things she had in the past, despite trying so hard. Eventually it became too much for her to bear. She asked my opinion about whether or not she should quit. I asked if the cons outweighed the benefits. To which she said, "I can't stand it so much that sometimes I just put my face in the water and scream." She was both frustrated and sad. I told her that if it was that upsetting to her, I agreed that it was probably time to let the swimming go for now.

Academically she was doing well. She worked tirelessly to do the absolute best she could in all of her courses. She had established some provisions with her teachers. Because she was unable to write, she had the help of note-takers in each class. She also was allowed double-time testing, as her brain injury had not only taken away her fine-motor coordination but also caused her to move slower now. When taking tests she went to the Office of Disability Services where she was allowed twice the normal time allotted to complete the test. This system worked out well for Alicia; eventually she found that extra time was not necessary in certain courses.

After much thought and seeking the advice of counselors in each of the schools of study, Alicia decided to change her major from early childhood education to social work; then she decided to focus on rehabilitation services, a major Wright State offered. She had to add several extra courses in order to make the change in her major but felt it would be worth it. Rehabilitation services seemed to be a better fit.

Developing new friendships was always an exciting part of life for Alicia, and she continued to do that each semester. She became more involved with a couple of student organizations and then focused most of that attention on the Circle K Club, which was very active in carrying out community service activities.

During that time she met her first real love, Adam, an engineering major. As he and Alicia grew closer, he used his inventive mind to come up with ways to help Alicia do activities she would otherwise not have been able to do. He regularly helped her practice walking up and down the walkway outside the dorm. They often went to the park or for a hike. He would carry her on his back to get wherever they needed to be. She finally had a chance to enjoy the outdoors, which she hadn't been able to do since her injury. They gradually became a couple and spent a lot of time together; eventually they stayed with family on weekends and during holidays. They thrived in their relationship and became engaged after almost two years. They stayed very active together in the clubs that they were involved in, spending weekends working on a variety of community service projects, as well as helping out at the local humane society.

Any relationship includes areas that need work. It was no different with this young couple. Alicia reacted to some changes in the relationship and got nervous. Because of her many limitations, she was conscious that she may not have been allowing him to do things he had enjoyed previously.

Being young and inexperienced in the art of negotiation, these two great kids had difficulty sorting through their thoughts and feelings. It developed into a tumultuous time, and as tensions elevated, the wonderful relationship that they shared spiraled downward. The two young adults who seemed to have been meant for each other went their separate ways.

Have you ever had a circumstances in your life that, if you had a chance to do over, everything would have been different? That was one of those situations for Alicia, one of her eternal regrets. She always will mourn the loss of her first real love, the man she thought was meant for her.

Alicia with Friends from Wright State University

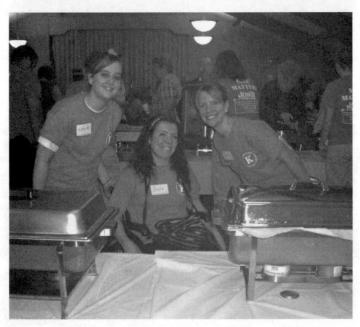

CHAPTER 21

Changing the World

THERE ARE ONLY TWO WAYS TO
LIVE YOUR LIFE.
ONE IS AS THOUGH NOTHING IS A MIRACLE.
THE OTHER AS THOUGH
EVERYTHING IS A MIRACLE.
~Albert Einstein~

YEAR AFTER YEAR THE VILLAGE STRIDERS chose to include Alicia as a recipient of their time and generosity. The September Wine-Tasting Social continues to this day, and an enormous number of people have been fortunate to receive the gifts lavished on them by the Village Striders.

In 2006 Alicia was told that she would again be one of the individuals to benefit from the Strider's fundraising event. At that point she was in school at Wright State and truly believed that she had everything she needed. She loved school and was able to eat and actively pursue her interests and dreams. Life was good.

Over the previous year or so, Alicia had become something of a social activist, becoming very passionate about the plight of disabled children around the world. She had been reading about how young people had to deal with physical limitations on a daily basis, especially in poorer countries of the world.

As the Village Striders were planning their fundraising event for that fall, Alicia made a diligent search for an organization that would be able to help with her desire to get wheelchairs to children in some of the poorer countries in Africa.

She identified several groups that worked to provide such young people with wheelchairs. After researching the various groups and how their organizations were run, as well as who was the most generous in getting the chairs to the people in need, Alicia chose to speak with someone within the Wheels for the World organization run by Joni Eareckson Tada. Wheels for the World is part of a larger organization called Joni and Friends, an organization that provides worldwide Christian outreach and encouragement to individuals with disabilities, as well as their families.

Phone calls were made and emails sent that connected with members of Wheels for the World. Alicia then announced to the Striders that the money raised that year would be donated to that organization. The Striders were 100-percent on board with that idea and welcomed Alicia's desire to reach out in love.

Joni Eareckson Tada's group was touched by Alicia's generosity. They invited Alicia, myself and Berta Andrulis, one of the founders of the Village Striders, to their international headquarters in Agoura Hills, California. At their annual board of director's meeting Alicia presented a check in the amount of $3,500 to Wheels for the World. The trip was wonderful; we all had a great time.

After receiving so much from so many, Alicia couldn't help but pass on the love and concern to others. Approximately twenty children were fitted for and provided with wheelchairs that they otherwise never would have had. For those children, a life of immobility and inability to participate was transformed into one of increased function, freedom, and hope in their daily lives. Pay it forward with love; it changes the world.

Alicia presenting the check to Joni Earecksen Tada to help the Wheels for the World Ministry. The Money was raised by the Village Striders in the fall of 2006.

Berta, Alicia, myself and Joni E. Tada at the annual Board of Directors meeting in Agoura Hills, CA in December 2006

Alicia and Berta ~ In the Pacific Ocean

Enjoying our trip to Agoura Hills

CHAPTER 22

Touching the Wall

MAKE NO SMALL PLANS. FOR THEY
HAVE NO POWER TO STIR THE SOUL
~Niccolo Machiavelli~

ALICIA DECIDED TO REMAIN IN OHIO for the summer
between her junior and senior year. She took a course
during each of the two summer sessions. She was enjoying college life and wanted to make sure that she had all
the credits she needed to graduate.

I went out to help her rearrange a few things and then
brought her back home for a couple of weeks before the
beginning of the fall semester of her senior year. It was
a time to catch up, enjoy each other's company, and assess
first-hand how her life had changed in the past five years.
Challenges and struggles remained, but Alicia had accomplished so much and had negotiated the turns in her new
life remarkably well. I was extremely proud of her—what
an amazingly strong young woman she had grown to be.

Her senior year seemed to fly by, filled with a variety
of activities. She carried a full academic load, did her
practicum at a rehab facility and remained quite involved
in the Circle K Club.

The winter of her senior year we were hit by one winter storm after another, most coming to us from the Midwest. I worried a bit about how Alicia would be able to get around in her wheelchair. She assured me that she could get rides on the campus shuttle if need be and pointed out that the maintenance department was very efficient in clearing the sidewalks and roads.

One afternoon she called me. "Hey, Ma, I have to tell you about something." She'd been on her way back from class when her wheelchair tire got caught in a groove on the sidewalk; she and the chair went off the curb and landed in a pile of snow. My heart sank, anxious about how she could deal with such a challenge.

She said that she fell out of the chair, and it had landed on her. I cringed! Her wheelchair was a very large model, with all manner of features, weighing just over four hundred pounds.

"Are you okay? What happened? Did anyone help you?" the anxiety building.

"No, there was no one around at first, so I pushed it off me with my legs and got it upright. Someone came along and helped me get it back on the sidewalk and helped me on."

"Are you all right?" I asked.

"Yeah, I'm fine, Ma."

I was just this side of frantic and said something along the lines of, "I'm glad to hear you are okay, but I hate to hear stories like that. It makes me nervous picturing you out there all by yourself."

To which Alicia replied, "That's why I told you, to show you I can totally take care of myself. I'm fine, Ma!"

Wow...I got it!

Later in her senior year, Alicia started dating a young man named Matthew. The relationship became more serious as time went on. As she was wrapping up her time in Ohio before returning home, they decided to take things by ear.

As the last quarter flew by, we planned our trip out to Ohio for the graduation. Crissy, Paul and I made our way to Ohio to see Alicia graduate. Bryan would not be able to attend, as he was a Marine stationed at Camp LeJeune, North Carolina. Although we didn't say so outright, our pride in and happiness for Alicia, and all that she had been through and accomplished, brought immense joy to our hearts.

On the day of the ceremony we arrived early and entered the E.J. Nutter Concert Center, where the ceremony was taking place. Matthew and I accompanied Alicia to the staging area downstairs. We took lots of pictures with Alicia and some of her friends, then I made my way back to find Paul and Crissy, who had found us excellent seats.

As I finally sat down and looked around, it hit me. Alicia had done it. Against all odds, with challenges at every turn, in a body that she was only still growing to recognize, she did it.

My beautiful daughter, who always tried to do what was right, who loved and cared for others unconditionally, got it all back. She had been surrounded those last years by love, given freely to her by so many. All of us wanted so much to help Alicia realize her dreams.

On graduation day Alicia was able to wheel herself to the front of the hall to receive her diploma along with her fellow graduates. She had accomplished her goal! On November 20, 2009, Alicia graduated with honors from

Wright State University in Dayton, Ohio, with a Bachelor of Science degree in rehabilitation services.

We stood and clapped for all of the graduates, but our love and pride was focused on the young woman who had overcome the impossible, who had changed all of our lives—the one who is our hero!

CHAPTER 23

Through Alicia's Eyes

CHALLENGES ARE WHAT MAKES LIFE INTERESTING,
OVERCOMING THEM IS WHAT MAKES LIFE MEANINGFUL.
~Joshua Marine~

A DRASTIC LIFE CHANGE WAS PROBABLY the last possibility I had imagined as an outcome of the surgery. I honestly was not all that worried. I had two minor concerns: first, the amount of school I would miss and how I would catch up with all my work, and second, what if the anesthesia didn't work? Those were the thoughts that continuously loomed in my mind. I also had rare moments when negative thoughts would hit me. My concerns mostly had to do with swimming and whatever changes might impact my life, but complications never really crossed my mind. I vaguely remember that I had the dream about my grandfather's death while I was in the hospital, so certain possibly worrisome issues had come up, but nothing close to what actually happened!

On the morning of surgery I sat in the waiting room and was then taken to the prep area; the last thing I remember was getting anesthesia. My memories of what happened after that are distorted and sparse. I was in

ICU, and the TV was on. My vision was very blurry; I had a headache and was throwing up. That was the last actual event I remember for quite awhile.

For a while I had "dreams," I guess you could call them, and actually remember several of them. In one "dream" I was in the basement of Yale, but in a hospital bed. All the monitors and things were there, as were nurses and random people. It was very dark, though, so I couldn't actually make out faces. My favorite soap opera was on. I remember watching quite a bit of that, though I don't recall anything that went on in the show. The other things I remember are just bits and pieces. The remainder of the "dreams" took place when I was upstairs, I guess. It was always pretty dark in whatever room I was in. The only exception was a time I was in a room on the children's unit. Because of the windows it was very bright. I remember my mom had this cot-type thing against the wall in front of me, under the windows. I vaguely remember one of my friends Megan Shove visited me and we watched *E.T* together. I also remember a little Asian nurse. I recall watching a band play, some of the nurses and some minor events. That was mostly it from Yale.

At Blythedale, all I remember accurately is the bright blue color of the walls. Now, this is where it gets weird for me… I remember going to physical and occupational therapy, but the therapists were entirely different people. I also sort of remember going to the cafeteria at times, watching certain TV shows, a roommate I had there, and some nurses that weren't very nice. Then my "dreams" go back to being in Yale. One weird thing I dreamed was that my mother and I were locked in at a house in New Haven. The challenge I was determined to overcome then was to get back home. I don't remember whether or not we accomplished that. The last "dream" I had before I "woke up" was a respiratory therapist banging on my back; there was a sign on the window.

The next thing I remember was looking up and seeing my eye lashes. It was brighter and more noisy than usual. My mother and my aunt were there, and the TV was on. I remember everything from then on. Not very well anymore, but I realized I was awake for good. Initially, the changes didn't really sink in, I guess. That first day my neurosurgeon, Dr. Duncan, came in and said there were some complications and that I would need to stay in the hospital for awhile longer. I wasn't able to talk at all, but that didn't come as a real shock for some reason. I kind of figured it was a small, temporary complication. We established a way of communicating; I would spell out words by nodding for each letter. I asked my mother a lot of questions; one of the first was "What is the date?" I believe it was May 21st. Until I learned the date, I was under the assumption that the dreams had occurred in a matter of four days. Before my surgery I was told that I would be in the hospital for that long. Until then, I was mostly worried that my scar would show when I did my hair for my junior prom. Obviously, I had missed that, along with the remainder of my junior year.

Everything all slowly started to make sense, but the real impact on my life wasn't quite resonating with me. After I learned all this, I really wanted to see myself in the mirror for some reason. I looked horrible! One eye was very red and turned in, and my hair was all shaved on the right side of my head. For whatever reason it wasn't really affecting me at the time…if that makes sense; maybe I was in shock? I couldn't tell you what was really going through my mind at the time. Everything was pretty much explained to me, in time; maybe the gradual realizations softened the blow.

In order to be accepted into Gaylord I had to be able to move my limbs a certain amount, so that became my goal for a while. I practiced and pushed myself for about a week prior to being evaluated for admittance to Gaylord. It was pretty painful and definitely challenging, but I was determined to get back to the way I was. At that time I was still convinced that my condition was just temporary and if I worked hard enough, I could easily return to my "normal" life.

After finally being discharged from Gaylord, I continued to simply take things in stride. By that point, I had come to grips with what had happened, and I was aware that my life would never be the same. I still did what I had to do, determined to get at least as close to "normal" as I could. I never really dealt with what had happened, though, and didn't really get upset until months or maybe even years later.

I continued outpatient physical, occupational and speech therapies. I went back to school, not in the most conventional way, but I did what I had to do to finish high school. I was determined! When they offered to graduate me with my class in 2003, I had to refuse. It didn't seem fair for me to do the least amount of work possible, and I felt that I would miss out on the stuff we learned during senior year. My ultimate goal was to go to college, and it didn't seem logical to skip a whole year's worth of schoolwork and learning if I planned on accomplishing that goal! So I continued from where I left off; which meant I'd be with a different class. For the most part that was okay, but I missed the people in the class I started high school with. Students in my new class

(2004) were mostly all very supportive and accepting, but things were often awkward. It was clear to me that those kids mostly just felt bad for me; they wouldn't have been so friendly otherwise. I made a few friends and was just pitied by the other students. It didn't bother me that much. I had other concerns.

Once I graduated from Holy Cross High School, I went out to college in Ohio in 2004. I was too homesick, so I only lasted for one quarter out there. I came back to Southern Connecticut State University, which was about forty minutes away from my home. I lived on campus, but being able to come home on the weekends was enough to relieve all my homesickness after about a year and a half. I then went back out to Wright State University, in Ohio. I completed my college years out there. Being out there pretty much by myself was definitely challenging, but fortunately I lucked out in the friend and boyfriend departments. I actually liked having to be fairly independent, and I accepted each new challenge. They taught me how to do things for myself and not to rely as much on other people. After I broke up with my boyfriend and my helpful friends graduated or transferred, my independence really had to take over. The last few months were more challenging for me. In November 2009, I graduated with a bachelor's degree in rehabilitation services, ready for the next chapter in life.

Epilogue

"Life isn't about waiting for the storm to pass,
It's about learning to dance in the rain."
~Vivian Greene~

LIFE FOR ALICIA SINCE 2002 has been about acceptance, it has been about perseverance and it has been about giving and receiving love. Her challenges are a daily occurrence; life has not been easy for her. She is no longer able to do many of the things that she once enjoyed.

Alicia continues to dream though. Many times over the years she has spoken about walking in her dreams, and has been doing that again recently. We have lightly pointed out how this may be a sign. One thing is for sure, it is evidence of an ever-present hope, a hope to one day live without her many limitations. What joy that would bring her!

She continues to work diligently for breakthroughs in the areas of physical therapy, particularly walking, communication through clarity of speech and progress with fine motor ability and coordination. She has resumed out-patient therapies at Gaylord Hospital twice a week.

Since graduation Alicia has sent out scores of resumes and had multiple job interviews. She made her way back to Ohio for several months in search of an entry level rehabilitation services position, eventually returning to Connecticut in order to take courses toward her Master's degree. Alicia inquired about the programs at Southern Connecticut State University, as well as at Wright State, and was mulling through the pros and cons of each. She also had been reconsidering her area of study, thinking through the advantages of pursuing a Master's degree in special education after speaking with friends and counselors in both fields.

In the fall of 2010 Alicia started to take special education courses at Southern Connecticut State University, with the intention of completing her Master's degree there, but her plans went on hold when she discovered that she was pregnant. She stopped school immediately, anticipating a complicated pregnancy. High-risk neonatologists at Yale New Haven Hospital followed her pregnancy closely.

On July 8, 2011, after a short but complicated labor Alicia delivered Liam, a healthy baby boy in the Maternal Special Care Unit at Yale New Haven Hospital. With all the potential problems considered, she gave birth in a room packed with high-risk neonatologists, pediatricians and nurses, as well as Crissy, myself and Matthew.

Liam has been a gift of love and joy to all of us. Interestingly enough, he was born three floors below the Pediatric Intensive Care Unit (PICU) where his mother had clung to life nine years before. Liam's middle name Duncan is a Celtic name, but more importantly was given to him in honor of Dr. Charles Duncan, the neurosurgeon who saved his mother's life.

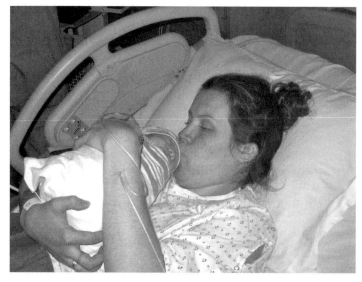

Alicia and Liam

Wisdom and peace are found in accepting what is, not in asking why. Strength is found in community, where we surround one another with love, accept each other as we are, call each other to be and do more, and share our gifts with one another. This is how we grow. This is how we change the world.

SPECIAL ACKNOWLEDGEMENT

FOUR VERY CLOSE FRIENDS OF OURS, individuals who made an amazing difference in the outcome of Alicia's story, have since passed away. These four wonderful individuals—Peg Andrulis, Fr. Stan Kennedy, Joanne McCormick, and Ellen Olschefski—demonstrated amazing support for Alicia, as well as our entire family, during the most trying of times for us. They are each truly missed. We will never forget them for all that they have done for Alicia, myself and our family, as well as the countless others whose lives they touched during theirs.

TIME IS TOO SLOW FOR THOSE WHO WAIT,
TOO SWIFT FOR THOSE WHO FEAR,
TOO LONG FOR THOSE WHO GRIEVE,
TOO SHORT FOR THOSE WHO REJOICE
...BUT FOR THOSE WHO LOVE,
TIME IS ETERNITY.
~Henry Van Dyke~

WE HAVE FOUND THE FOLLOWING organizations to be invaluable as resources in assisting us with our needs as well as in providing ideas at the time of Alicia's sudden and life-changing illness.

I hope that you will find them helpful as well, if you ever have a need for such services.

I also encourage you to contact any of these organizations to see how you may be able to contribute to their ongoing missions.

Angel Flight
www.angelflight.org
Arrange free flights so children and adults can access medical care.(There are multiple websites, depending on your location in the US)

www.angelflight.com (services primarily to the Heartland)

www.angelflightne.org (services to the Northeast United States)

Brain Injury Association of America
1608 Spring Hill Rd., Suite 110, Vienna, VA. 22182
761-0750
www.biausa.org

Brain Injury Support Group on FaceBook
http:/supportforbraininjuries

Brain Injury Resource Center
www.headinjury.com
(206) 621-8558
PO Box 84151, Seattle, WA 98125-5451
Promotes proactive involvement, knowledge, self-awareness, and self-advocacy following a brain injury

Brainline.org
Preventing, treating, and living with traumatic brain injuries. Providing resources for persons with TBIs and family, friends, and professionals.
Resource directory, personal stories, research updates

Caring Bridge
www.caringbridge.org/howwehelp
A nonprofit online service set up to help any family going through a health event. Allows each family and support group a safe, personal space to communicate information to a wide circle of people. They can post on daily journals, and the guestbook allows visitors to send the family messages of love and encouragement.

Centers for Independent Living, United States
http://www.ilusa.com/links/ilcenters.htm

Centerwatch
http://www.centerwatch.com/
CenterWatch is the leading trusted source for global clinical trial information.

Circle of Care
www.thecircleofcare.org
Providing support and resources to families of children with cancer.

Clinicaltrials.gov
A registry of publicly and privately supported studies of human participants conducted around the world: a service of the National Institutes of Health (NIH).

Daily Strength: Brain Injury Online Support Group.
www.dailystrength.org
A network of people sharing their knowledge, experience, and support for a number of medical conditions, through online support groups: making friends, journaling, tracking goals, sharing...

Disabled-Friendly Universities
http://www.collegexpress.com/lists/list/the-experts-choice-colleges-that-are-particularly-able-to-accommodate-a-student-in-a-wheelchair/402/

Rehabilitation Hospitals

Gaylord Hospital – Connecticut
http://www.gaylord.org/

Blythedale Children's Hospital – Valhalla, NY
www.blythedale.org

Hospital for Special Care – Connecticut
http://hfsc.org/

(*U.S News & World Reports* List of Best Rehabilitation Hospitals in the US)
http://health.usnews.com/best-hospitals/rankings/
  rehabilitation

Ronald McDonald House
www.rmh-ct.org
(Links to all Ronald McDonald House online resources)

Housing provided throughout the United States and internationally, offering a home away from home for families of children being treated at nearby hospitals or health care facilities.

Wheels for the World Charity
http://www.joniandfriends.org/wheels-for-the-world/

These sources have been helpful to us and countless others. Never stop searching for what you need!

A Heartfelt Thank You

TO THE MANY PEOPLE WHO have touched our lives with kindness and love in our time of need. Your prayers, thoughtfulness and generosity have been greatly appreciated. The ongoing support from so many groups and individuals has overwhelmed us. We are convinced that Alicia would not have progressed so well were it not for the love and prayers of so many. We have felt truly blessed to be part of such a caring community.

Alicia's Family

Campion Ambulance Service
Expressly Fit
Gaylord Hospital – Hooker II Staff and Therapy Dept.
Holy Cross Girls Swim Team
Holy Cross Girls Track Team
Holy Cross High School – Administration, Staff and
    Students
Knights of Columbus Pius X Council
Litchfield Parks & Recreation
Middlebury Fire Dept.
Republican-American Newspaper
Ronald McDonald Houses in New Haven and Cleveland
St. John the Evangelist Parish Family
St. Mary's Hospital friends and co-workers
Stone Construction Co
The Village Striders of Litchfield

UNICO of Watertown
Veterans Who Care Committee
Watertown Age Group Swim Team
Watertown High School Girl's Swim Team
Watertown Lions Club
Watertown Parks & Recreation
Watertown United Methodist Church
Yale New Haven Children's Hospital – (Staff - PICU,
    School Age Unit and 7-4)
Loyal and caring friends, the best family in the world
and all others who have shown their support in a variety
of ways.

This 'Thank You' appeared in several local papers in the
fall of 2002. We remain forever grateful!

Order Form

Email orders: ceitinn13@yahoo.com
or
cceitinn57@msn.com

Telephone orders: 860-417-9041

Postal orders: Ceitinn Press
P.O. Box 1321
Middlebury, CT 06762

Please send the following number of books:_____

I understand that I may return any of them for a full refund, for any reason, if in unopened condition.

Name:_____

Mailing Address:_____

_____

City, State/province, Zip Code: _____

_____

Telephone:(   ) _____

Email: _____

Payments accepted : Check or PayPal

KEEP IN TOUCH

We invite and encourage you to keep in touch with us. Please feel free to offer comments, ask any questions, request speaking engagements or just say hello through any of our on-line sites.

Send an email : ckeating@todanceintherain.com

Become a fan on Facebook: To Dance in the Rain
https://www.facebook.com/pages/To-Dance-in-the-Rain/155687617965563

Follow us on Twitter : ceitinn.13clare

**Keep up on book news weekly on our blogs,
through our website:**

www.todanceintherain.com

**See our website for information
on resources, speaking engagements
and mailing lists and more**.

Never the End…
Love Lives Forever !